FRIENDS OF THE EARTH

A History of American Environmentalism

PAT MCCARTHY

CHICAGO REVIEW PRESS

Copyright © 2013 by Pat McCarthy
First edition
Published by Chicago Review Press, Incorporated
814 North Franklin Street
Chicago, Illinois 60610
ISBN 978-1-56976-718-4

Unless otherwise noted, all photos have been taken by the author.

Library of Congress Cataloging-in-Publication Data

McCarthy, Pat, 1940-
  Friends of the earth : a history of American environmentalism / Pat McCarthy. — 1st ed.
     p. cm.
  ISBN 978-1-56976-718-4 (pbk.)
 1. Environmentalism—United States--History—Juvenile literature. 2. Environmentalists—United States—History—Juvenile literature. 3. Environmental protection—United States—History—Juvenile literature. I. Title.

 GE197.M35 2012
 304.2092'273—dc23
                        2012039334

Cover design: Jonathan Hahn
Cover photos counterclockwise from left: Red-bellied woodpecker, Shutterstock © Elliotte Rusty Harold; Thoreau, Library of Congres LC-USZ61-361; Julia Butterfly Hill, Time & Life Pictures/Getty Images © John Storey; Grand Teton National Park, [TK Flickr]; Rachel Carson, Time & Life Pictures/Getty Images © Time Life Pictures; bird in the Everglads, Ken Pomerance © MrClean Photography; John Muir, Library of Congress LC-B2- 1309-10.
Interior design: Sarah Olson
Interior Illustations: Mark Baziuk

Printed in the United States of America
5 4 3 2 1

To my great-grand niece and nephews
Carson, Madison, Kolton, and Blake Gray

CONTENTS

TIME LINE

William Penn

Henry David Thoreau

Gifford Pinchot

1690 William Penn requires settlers to preserve one acre of trees for every five acres cleared

1739 Benjamin Franklin petitions Pennsylvania Assembly to stop industries from dumping waste

1827 First volume of Audubon's *Birds of America* is published

1845 Thoreau builds his cabin at Walden Pond

1849 Department of the Interior is created

1854 Thoreau's *Walden* is published

1868 John Muir first sees the Yosemite Valley

1890 Yosemite National Park is created

1891 The Forest Reserve Act is passed

1892 The Sierra Club is founded

1898 Gifford Pinchot is named head of the Division of Forestry

1905 The National Audubon Society is founded

Cordelia Stanwood begins her systematic observations of nesting birds

1910	Cordelia Stanwood begins publishing her nesting bird studies
1934	Roger Tory Peterson creates his bird identification system
1935	The Wildnerness Society is formed
1947	Marjory Stoneman Douglas's *River of Grass* is published
	Everglades National Park is created
1949	Aldo Leopold's *Sand County Almanac* is published
1960	Arctic National Wildlife Reserve is created, due to efforts by Mardie and Olaus Murie
1962	Rachel Carson's *Silent Spring* is published
1964	The Wilderness Act is passed
1970	The Clean Air Act is passed
	The first Earth Day is observed
	The Environmental Protection Agency is created
1989	The *Exxon Valdez* oil spill occurs in Alaska
2006	Al Gore's *An Inconvenient Truth* is published
2011	The BP oil spill occurs in the Gulf of Mexico

Cordelia Stanwood

Marjory Stoneman Douglas

Rachel Carson

INTRODUCTION

SAVING LUNA:
LIFE IN A GIANT REDWOOD

For 18 hours, the winds howled and the rain pelted down. Julia Butterfly Hill held onto her tree for dear life. Ninety-mile-per-hour winds tipped the six-by-eight-foot wooden platform on which she lived in the giant redwood tree. One gust actually blew her three feet off the platform. She managed to grab branches and hold on until she could make her way back. Julia said she learned from this storm that in order to survive, you have to quit fighting, bend with the wind, and go with the flow.

You're probably wondering why Hill was living in a tree. A year earlier, she had been critically injured in a car crash. It took her nearly a year to recover, and she used that time to consider what she believed was important in life. She took a trip west to try to decide what to do with her life.

Hill tells about her first sight of the ancient redwoods: "When I entered the majestic cathedral of the redwood forest for the first time, my spirit knew it had found what it was searching for. I dropped to my knees and began to cry because I was so overwhelmed by the wisdom, energy, and spirituality housed in this holiest of temples."

Hill had been horrified by the clear-cutting of redwoods in California. She was devastated when she saw her first redwoods being cut. She says, "I sobbed, screamed, raged, and cried because it hurt so. It was very painful." When she learned that only 3 percent of the giant redwoods remained, she decided to take action.

Hill and many others had tried to inform the American people of the problem. No one paid much attention. So when she heard that a group was looking for someone who would spend some time sitting in the giant redwood tree known as Luna, Julia volunteered.

On December 10, 1997, when Hill was 23 years old, she climbed high into Luna. She later said, "I gave my word to this tree and to all the people that my feet would not touch the ground until I had done everything in my power to make the world aware of this problem and to stop the destruction." She was there for a little over two years.

All around her, the Pacific Lumber Company was cutting trees. Hill said, "You hear the incessant buzzing of the chain saws hour after hour until your ears are ringing, and then you hear the creaking, the groaning as it's about to fall and then it sounds like thunder as it crashes through all the trees it has to hit on the way down and then it's a loud BWAAM-BOOM! You can feel the earth trembling all the way up through Luna."

The lumber company had posted security guards at the base of the tree. At first they blew bugles and air horns at night to keep her from sleeping and called her names and cussed at her. They also tried to keep her from getting supplies.

Hill's home for two years was that six-by-eight-foot wooden platform. Her walls and roof were made out of tarps. She had a single-burner camp stove to cook on and a cell phone to stay in touch with other environmental workers. Solar panels placed in the tree powered the phone.

Her friends used a rope to send up supplies, including food, mail, and propane for the stove. For a bathroom, she used a bucket, then put the waste in a plastic bag and lowered it to the ground. Her friends took it away and disposed of it properly.

For exercise, Hill climbed around in the tree and walked around the platform. She collected rainwater in the tarps to use for cooking, bathing, and drinking.

Finally, on December 18, 1999, Hill received good news. The Pacific Lumber Company had agreed never to cut down Luna. They also agreed that they would not log any other trees in a three-acre area around it. So Hill ended her two-year tree sit. She and other environmentalists had raised $50,000, which they gave to the logging company to be used for research on sustainable forestry.

Julia Butterfly Hill received several awards for her bravery and determination. She continues to work to save the forests, including rainforests in South and Central America.

ENVIRONMENTALISM THROUGH THE YEARS

So what is environmentalism, and when did it begin? *Environmentalism* means working to take care of our Earth and to solve problems such as the pollution of water and air and the exhaustion of natural resources. Many people think environmentalism is a new idea, developed within the past 50 years or so.

However, American environmentalism began before the Europeans arrived in the Americas. They didn't call it environmentalism, but the Native Americans practiced it. When they killed an animal, they didn't waste any part of it. The meat of buffalo was used for food, the skin for clothing and tepees, the fat for making candles, and the bone to make tools.

American Indians had a reverence for their environment. They believed that man was a part of his environment and that all things in the environment were related to one

William Penn. *Dover Publications, Inc.*

another. Curley Bear Wagner, cultural officer for the Montana Blackfeet, said, "Your environmental movement is just white people beginning to put down roots on this continent. It's about time."

Like all other cultural groups, Native Americans at times misused the land, overhunted game, and overpopulated certain areas. However, they paid a great deal of attention to the environment compared with other cultural groups.

The European settlers in America made some early attempts at caring for the environment. William Penn, governor of Pennsylvania in 1690, required the settlers there to preserve one acre of trees for every five acres they cleared. In 1739, Benjamin Franklin petitioned the Pennsylvania Assembly to stop industries from dumping waste. When Franklin died in 1789, he left money in his will to build a pipeline to take fresh water to the city of Philadelphia because the polluted water there was causing disease.

A few other steps toward saving the environment were taken before 1850. In 1832, Arkansas Hot Springs was established as a national reservation. The same year, author and artist George Caitlin suggested the idea of national parks to preserve both the wilderness and the land the American Indians lived on. The US Department

American Indians Speak About the Environment

"The survival of the world depends upon our sharing what we have and working together. If we don't, the whole world will die. First the planet, and next the people."
—**Frank Fools Crow**, Ceremonial Chief of the Teton Sioux

"We must protect the forests for our children, grandchildren, and children yet to be born. We must protect the forests for those who can't speak for themselves such as the birds, animals, fish, and trees."
—**Qwatsinas** (Hereditary Chief Edward Moody)

"Treat the earth well; it was not given to you by your parents, it was loaned to you by your children. We do not inherit the earth from our ancestors, we borrow it from our children."
—**Ancient Indian Proverb**

"When we Indians kill meat, we eat it all up. When we dig roots, we make little holes. When we build houses, we make little holes . . . we don't ruin things. We shake down acorns and pine nuts. We don't chop down the trees. We use only dead wood."
—**Winter Woman**, 19th century

of the Interior was created in 1849. Its purpose was to manage the United States' national and cultural resources.

From 1850 to 1960, environmentalism was mostly concerned with conservation and preservation. For years, conservationists worked for efficient use and development of national resources. They tried to use these resources wisely so they would continue to be available.

Many national parks were established during those years. John Muir and President Theodore Roosevelt were both instrumental in establishing parks. The Forest Reserve Act was passed in 1891. This act gave the president authority to put public land into forest preserves.

Organizations were formed to protect the environment. In 1892, John Muir and Robert Underwood Johnson founded the Sierra Club. Chapters of the National Audubon Society began in New York and Massachusetts in 1896. Most of the early environmentalists who belonged to these clubs were mainly interested in preserving wilderness to be used for recreation.

Gifford Pinchot, the first American with a degree in forest management, believed in using our resources wisely while taking steps to conserve and replace these resources for later use. He and John Muir became friends, but their friendship ended in 1897. Muir's aim was to preserve the wilderness, rather than use any of its resources. This began the split between the conservationists, led by Pinchot, and the preservationists, led by Muir.

Theodore Roosevelt and John Muir.
*Library of Congress
LC-US262-8672*

The focus of environmentalism began to change in the 1960s. Now people were concerned about pollution, chemicals, and oil spills. Rachel Carson's book *Silent Spring* ushered in the new era in 1962. Carson showed that scientific progress had put Americans in peril from pollution. She showed that people's health was in danger because of the careless disposal of factory wastes and the use of pesticides. Scientists tried to

BUILD A COMPOST PILE

Things grow well on the forest floor because leaves and plants die and decay there, enriching the soil. Meanwhile, landfills are filling up. You can keep garbage out of the landfills and help your plants grow better at the same time.

WHAT YOU NEED

- A place in the yard not too close to the house
- Garden hose
- Twigs and leaves
- Garbage such as grass clippings and fruit and vegetable waste
- Shovel
- Soil

WHAT YOU DO

1. Use a garden hose to wet the ground where you want your compost pile to be.

2. Put a layer of leaves and twigs at the bottom. This will help add oxygen to the pile.

3. Add grass clippings, weeds, and fruit and vegetable waste. Do NOT include meat scraps, bones, dairy products, or oily foods. These things will smell bad and may attract mice.

4. Add some soil to the pile. Worms will live in this layer and help break up the compost.

5. Put more dead leaves, small twigs, or hay on top.

6. After a few days, your pile will be warm inside. Use your shovel to turn the pile every few days. If it seems dry, add a little water.

7. Keep adding fruit and vegetable waste, leaves, and grass cuttings.

8. It will take several months for your compost to change to soil that you can use in your garden.

Compost pile.

convince the public that Carson was a hysterical woman who was overreacting.

Several catastrophes during the 1960s made people realize that the environment was indeed at risk. First came the 1968 garbage strike in New York City. Before it was settled, 100,000 tons of rotting garbage lay in doorways and along the streets, waiting to be picked up. Health authorities feared an epidemic of typhoid or another disease. Luckily the strike ended before that could happen.

In 1969, the Cuyahoga River near Cleveland, Ohio, caught fire. It was actually an oil slick and the debris floating on the river that burned. The fire only lasted half an hour, and it did just $50,000 worth of damage. But it made the public aware that pollution was a major problem.

That same year, there was an oil spill in Santa Barbara, California. Over 200,000 gallons of crude oil spilled into the ocean, covering 800 square miles of the surface. Thirty-five miles of coastline were affected, and thousands of birds and other animals died. It took 11 days to stop the leak.

Disasters like these convinced the American people that they faced significant environmental problems. Congress passed four pieces of legislation to help. The Wilderness Act, passed in 1964, defined *wilderness* as "an area where the earth and its community of life are untrammeled [not disturbed] by man, where man himself is a visitor who does not remain." In these areas, no vehicles would be allowed, no permanent structures could be built, and the wildlife and its environment would be protected.

(*left*) President Richard Nixon. *Library of Congress LC-USZ62-13037*

(*right*) Girl Scout picking trash out of the Potomac River on the first Earth Day, 1970. *Library of Congress LC-DIG-ds-00750*

In 1968 the National Trails Act set up a system of national trails. The first of these were the Appalachian Trail and the Pacific Crest National Scenic Trail. The act created the trails to provide outdoor recreation opportunities and to promote the preservation of outdoor areas. The Wild and Scenic Rivers Act the same year safeguarded certain rivers for present and future generations to enjoy.

Some say the first Earth Day in 1970 marked the beginning of modern environmentalism. The Clean Air Act was passed in 1970. Its main purpose was to protect and improve the air quality in the United States in order to improve public health. Rallies all over the country convinced people that the environment was in danger. Also in 1970, President Nixon created the Environmental Protection Agency (EPA). The EPA's mission is to protect human health and the environment.

The 1970s brought more problems involving toxic chemicals. In the winter of 1973–74, an oil shortage brought about an energy crisis. In 1979, a meltdown at a nuclear reactor on Three Mile Island in Pennsylvania released radioactive steam into the air. People were terrified, but there was very little damage to the environment. However, the incident made people aware of the possible danger from nuclear plants.

During the 1980s, President Reagan's administration did little to further the environmental movement. He thought environmentalism was a threat to big business interests. Huge cuts were made in the budget of the EPA. More environmental groups sprang up in opposition to Reagan's policies. Some believed overpopulation was the biggest problem, while others blamed technology for causing pollution.

In recent years, some factories have had to find new ways to dispose of hazardous waste. This remains a problem in the 21st century.

Much has been done to improve the quality of air and water, but more work lies ahead. Oil spills continue to be a problem. Natural resources are being used up, and the need for alternative forms of energy is becoming critical. Rainforests continue to disappear at an alarming rate. Many species of plants and animals are losing their habitats. Global warming due to the greenhouse effect is a growing problem, and so is acid rain. In the last chapter, you'll find more about these problems and what is being done about them.

In the next 11 chapters, you'll meet 11 people who made a big difference in the environmentalist movement in the United States. These men and women dedicated their lives to saving our Earth. They worked in different ways and in different times and places, but they all made important contributions.

THE GREENHOUSE EFFECT

The Earth's climate has changed many times over the millennia. There have been ice ages and times when much of the planet was covered with subtropical forests. But now scientists say that people are changing the climate. Gases, such as carbon dioxide, are released when people burn fuels such as oil, gas, wood, and coal. These gases build up in the atmosphere and keep the heat in. This greenhouse effect has always kept the Earth at a comfortable temperature. However, now more of the gas is remaining in the atmosphere, causing it to get warmer.

This experiment will show you how the greenhouse effect works.

WHAT YOU NEED

- ❧ 2 identical large glass jars
- ❧ 4 cups cold water
- ❧ 10 ice cubes
- ❧ Plastic bag
- ❧ Thermometer

WHAT YOU DO

1. Pour 2 cups of water into each jar.

2. Put 5 ice cubes in each jar.

3. Seal one of the jars in a plastic bag. (This will show the greenhouse effect.)

4. Set the jars in the sun and let them sit for an hour.

5. Use a thermometer to measure the temperature of the water in each jar.

The temperature should be higher in the jar that was in the plastic bag. The bag acts like a greenhouse, letting in light and heat from the sun. The heat will have built up in this jar and not in the other.

JOHN JAMES AUDUBON
1785-1862

John James Audubon has come to be known as the man who familiarized people in the United States and Great Britain with the species of birds found in America.

Audubon was born in Santo Domingo (now Haiti) on April 26, 1785. His father, Lieutenant Jean Audubon, was a French sea captain. His mother was Jeanne Rabin, a Spanish Creole from Louisiana who lived on his father's sugar plantation. (Jean Audubon had a wife in France.) The baby was named Jean-Jacques Fougere Audubon. His mother died when he was an infant.

In 1788, slave uprisings forced Audubon to sell his plantation. He took the little boy and his younger half-sister, Rosa, to Nantes, France. His wife, Anne Moynet Audubon, raised them as her own. And in 1794, she legally adopted them.

John James Audubon. *Library of Congress LC-USZ62-11250*

Robin on nest.

Jean loved birds from an early age, and his father encouraged his interest. Jean said, "He would point out the elegant movement of the birds, and the beauty and softness of their plumage. He called my attention to their show of pleasure or sense of danger. . . . He would speak of their departure and return with the seasons." Jean often brought home birds' eggs and nests. He began to draw birds that he saw in France.

Jean's father was concerned about Jean's lack of interest in his studies, so he took him to the French naval base at Rochefort, where he was stationed. Here the boy studied with a tutor. Once, when he was given some difficult math problems, Jean jumped out the window into the gardens. However, a naval officer took him back to his room.

Lt. Audubon finally gave up and let Jean return home and attend school there. During that time, the boy made more of an effort to paint birds well. Also, to please his mother, he learned his catechism and was baptized.

Jean's first attempts at drawing birds were not good. He later wrote, "When I was a little lad, I first began my attempts at representing birds on paper, I was far from possessing much knowledge of their nature. . . . I was under the impression that it was a finished picture of a bird because it possessed some sort of a head and tail, and two sticks in lieu of legs." Since the boy showed little interest in anything else, his father encouraged him in his drawing.

Meanwhile, Napoleon began drafting young men into the army. In order to keep Jean from

Audubon later said, "Let no one speak of her as my step-mother. I was ever to her as a son of her own flesh and blood and she was to me a true mother." Mrs. Audubon treated the children well, although she spoiled the boy.

Jean's father was away from home a lot, and he left the childraising to his wife. Jean played the flute and the violin and liked to fence, ride, and dance.

He didn't like to go to school, so he often played hooky with other boys. They roamed the woods and fields, fishing, shooting, and hunting for birds' nests.

BUILD A BIRD NEST

In this activity, you will learn how birds' nests are made and try making one of your own.

WHAT YOU NEED

- Field guide of birds' nests or pictures of nests from the Internet
- Bowl
- Mud
- Small twigs
- Moss
- Hair—human, dog, cat, etc.
- Small pieces of yarn
- Feathers
- Leaves
- Dry grass
- Spoon

WHAT YOU DO

1. Study the birds' nests in the pictures or the field guide.

2. Pick a nest to make. Find out what size the nest should be for this bird. Look at the shape of the nest.

3. Fill a bowl with mud. Add water if it's too thick. You want it nice and sticky.

4. Use your materials to form a nest of the right shape and size. Add mud to hold the nest together.

5. Let your nest dry, then compare it with a real nest. Is yours as sturdy?

6. Scatter the leftover materials outside, where birds can pick them up to use in making their nests.

Mill Grove House, where Audubon lived when he came to America.
Library of Congress HABS PA,46-AUD,1A—1

Young men and women ice skating.
Library of Congress LC-USZ2629-91165

being drafted, his father sent him to America. Jean immediately changed his name to John James, the name he used the rest of his life.

John James was excited about the move. He enjoyed the trip, but when he reached New York, he became very ill with yellow fever. The ship's captain took him to two Quaker women who ran a boardinghouse. They nursed him back to health, and he later wrote, "To their skillful and untiring ministrations, I may safely say I owe . . . my life."

Soon he was established at Mill Grove, his father's farm in Pennsylvania. He lived with the Quaker tenants, William Thomas and his wife. Audubon loved life at Mill Grove. He wrote that Mill Grove was "refreshed by the waters of the Schuylkill River, and transversed by a creek named Perkioming. Its fine woodlands, its extensive acres, its fields crowned with evergreens, provided many subjects to my pencil."

Audubon was popular with the other young people in the area and spent his time enjoying himself. He was a great dancer, played the violin well, and was a good hunter. He said, "Hunting, fishing, drawing, and music occupied my every moment. Not a ball, a skating match, a house or a riding party took place without me."

Audubon dressed in satin pants, ruffled shirts, and silk stockings. He even dressed this way while hunting or roaming through the woods, finding birds and studying them. He wrote in his journal, "The nature of the place—whether high or low, moist or dry, whether sloping north or south, or bearing tall trees or low shrubs—generally gives hint as to its inhabitants." He spent a lot of time drawing the birds he found.

Soon after he arrived at Mill Grove, Audubon met a British neighbor, William Bakewell, in the woods. The man invited him to the house and Audubon was immediately enchanted by Bakewell's daughter, Lucy. He later wrote to his sons, "There I sat, my eyes riveted . . . on the

MAKE A RECYCLED BIRD FEEDER

You can make your own bird feeder from things around the house that you would otherwise throw away.

WHAT YOU NEED

Adult supervision required

- 2-liter pop bottle, empty
- Hobby knife
- 2 thin dowel rods, each 1 foot long
- Magic marker
- Black oil sunflower seeds
- Funnel
- Wire, 18 inches long

WHAT YOU DO

1. Wash out the 2-liter bottle and peel off the label.

2. Two inches up from the bottom, poke a hole large enough for a dowel to fit through.

3. Push the dowel straight across the inside of the bottle. Mark the place where it hits the side of the bottle.

4. Poke another hole at the mark and push the dowel through so it's sticking out both sides of the bottle. This will make two perches for the birds to sit on.

5. Halfway around the bottle and about ½ inch higher, poke a hole for the other dowel. Make a hole on the other side the same as you did for the first dowel. Push the dowel through. The two dowels will cross. Now you have four perches.

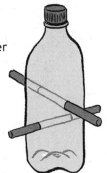

6. Above each perch, cut a small arch-shaped hole about an inch high and an inch wide.

7. Take the cap off the bottle. Use a funnel to fill it with sunflower seeds.

8. Wind a piece of wire several times around the top of the bottle below the cap. Make a loop out of the top of the wire. Use the loop to hang the feeder from a tree branch.

young girl before me, who half working, half talking, essayed to make the time pleasant to me. Oh! may God bless her! It was she, my dear sons, who afterwards became my beloved wife and your mother."

The two became great friends, and Lucy was with Audubon when he carried out a scientific experiment. He had discovered a phoebe's nest in a cave on the property. He wondered if the same birds would return the next year, so he carefully tied threads around their feet. The birds returned the next spring, still wearing the worn and dirty pieces of string on their legs. This was the first bird-banding experiment in the United States.

Audubon and Lucy were in love, but her parents thought they were too young to marry. Her father was also concerned that Audubon had no way to support her. John James was not a good businessman. Along with two other men, he reopened an old lead mine on the farm. The mine did contain lead, but it was expensive to reopen it and they made no profit.

Audubon went back to visit his parents in France. He wanted to get his father's permission to marry Lucy. He also met naturalist Charles-Marie D'Orbigny, who taught him the skill of taxidermy, or stuffing animals. This made it easier for Audubon to pose the birds he shot in order to draw them in lifelike positions.

Jean Audubon and a friend, François Rozier, got together and set up a business partnership for their two sons, John James and Ferdinand. Both boys were eager to get out of the country to avoid being drafted into the French Army. Jean managed to get passports for the boys and got them on an American ship, the *Polly*.

The two men sent a number of gold coins with the boys to use until they made a profit from their business. About two weeks after they left France, the *Polly* was overtaken by another ship, the British privateer *Rattlesnake*. Privateers were ships that were privately owned but were authorized by the government during wartime to attack and capture enemy vessels. The crew of the *Rattlesnake* took two crew members and much of the cargo, but didn't bother the passengers. John James and Ferdinand had hidden their gold pieces inside rolls of cable on deck. The privateers did not find the gold.

Audubon worked in Philadelphia for a while for Bakewell's brother, Benjamin. He was to learn the mercantile business, which was the business of buying and selling goods. Rozier worked for a French importing firm. Audubon also did some part-time work for Dr. Samuel Latham Mitchell, who was a leading naturalist in New York. He probably wasn't paid for this work. Audubon mounted animal specimens and prepared bird and animal skins for a museum. He did the work in his room, and the neighbors soon became upset at the unpleasant odors. The smell became so bad that they called the constable.

Eventually Audubon got tired of working for someone else. He wrote to Rozier on May 6, 1807, that he wanted to start a store. He had decided what goods they should carry and that the store would be in Kentucky.

Alexander Wilson

Audubon wasn't the first person to decide to paint all the birds of North America. Alexander Wilson had set out to do the same thing.

Alexander Wilson was born in Paisley, Scotland. He was called Sandy as child. His mother died when he was 10. When he was 12 or 13, he worked as an apprentice for his brother-in-law, William Duncan, who was a weaver.

Wilson was more interested in writing poetry than he was in weaving. After a few years with Duncan, Wilson became a peddler. Some of his poetry got him into trouble. He wrote a poem about how badly weaving apprentices were treated by their masters. He had to spend a short time in jail, then publicly burn the poem at the crossroads of the town.

In 1794, when he was 28, Wilson decided to leave Scotland to start a new life in America. His nephew, also named William Duncan, went with him. Duncan moved north to farm in New York State. Wilson spent years as a teacher in Pennsylvania and New Jersey.

When he moved to Gray's Ferry, Pennsylvania, to teach, he

Alexander Wilson. *Dover Publications, Inc.*

met naturalist William Bartram, who was his neighbor. Bartram ran the Bartram Botanical Gardens and got Wilson interested in birds.

In the early 1800s, Wilson decided to write a book depicting all the North American birds. He traveled widely, observing birds and painting them. In 1805 Wilson wrote a letter to President Thomas Jefferson. He volunteered his services as naturalist on a trip to explore land in the west. Though he was not asked to make the trip, he and Jefferson later became friends.

Wilson moved to Philadelphia, where he was assistant editor of *Ree's Cyclopedia*. The publisher, William Bradford, was impressed with his work and offered to back him in publishing the book. *American Ornithology* was published in nine volumes and showed 268 species of birds. Twenty-six of these species had never been described before. He described the behavior and habitat of each bird. The set of books sold for $120, which was more than he made in a year as a teacher.

Wilson traveled far and wide, selling subscriptions for the book. It was on one of these trips that he met Audubon in Louisville. Wilson mentioned in his journal that they went shooting.

The first volume of *American Ornithology* came out in 1808. Wilson was working on the final volume in 1813 when he died of dysentery. His friend George Ord finished the book for him.

Wilson is remembered as the greatest American ornithologist before Audubon. Three species of birds are named for him—Wilson's Phalarope, Wilson's Warbler, and Wilson's Storm Petrel.

The two young men made the long, hard trip to Kentucky. The country they passed through was beautiful. The boat slipped between high hills and heavy forests, sometimes passing a small settlement. They slept on their coats on deck at night.

The river presented a number of hazards. The boat sometimes got stuck on a sandbar, and all the passengers had to get into the water and push in order to free it. Sometimes rocks, dirt, and trees that had fallen into the water blocked their way.

The flatboat finally made it to Louisville. The town was located on a high bluff overlooking the Ohio River. Audubon and Rozier immediately explored the town, looking for a suitable building for their business. Audubon had no head for business, and Rozier didn't have much experience.

Even though the business wasn't very successful, Audubon returned to Pennsylvania in 1808, determined to marry Lucy. Her father finally agreed, and the two were married on April 5 in the parlor at Fatland Ford, the Bakewells' home.

Audubon took Lucy back with him to Louisville. He continued to tramp through the woods, drawing birds, while Rozier tended the store. Lucy gave birth to four children during their time in Kentucky. Victor Gifford was the oldest, then John Woodhouse. Two daughters died in infancy.

In 1810, Alexander Wilson came into the store while Audubon happened to be there. Wilson was trying to sell subscriptions to his book of bird pictures. Audubon wasn't overly impressed with his artwork.

Audubon had invented a new way of drawing birds. He shot them with fine shot so they wouldn't be torn to pieces. Then he used wires to prop them up in natural positions. He sometimes spent four 15-hour days preparing a single bird and drawing it. His birds were drawn in their natural habitat and were often in motion. Next to his pictures, the paintings of others, such as Alexander Wilson, seemed stiff.

And Audubon was a perfectionist. If he wasn't satisfied with his paintings, he would destroy them and do them over. Early in his career, 200 of Audubon's paintings were shredded by rats. He worked very hard redoing them.

For a while he was able to help support his family by doing black-and-white portraits for people. But by 1819, he had run out of people to draw and was thrown into jail for debt. After he got out, he tried to start a business in New Orleans, worked at a museum in Cincinnati, and lived on a plantation, where he taught drawing to the owner's young daughter. He also spent time roaming in the woods and working on paintings for his book.

Lucy was trained as a teacher, so she taught classes for children from the Audubons' home. Later she and the children lived on a plantation, where she taught the children of the family.

In 1824, Audubon was ready to find a publisher for his book. He went to Philadelphia, but he made enemies of some of the leading scientists at the Academy of Natural Sciences. He met Charles Lucien Bonaparte, a nephew of Napoleon. Charles was a famed French ornithologist living temporarily in the United States. He liked Audubon and was impressed with his work. He suggested he try to find a publisher in Europe.

Lucy and John James talked over the idea and decided he should try it. In 1826 he sailed from New Orleans, taking 300 drawings with him. He went to England, where he had letters of introduction to some prominent Englishmen. He traveled around the country with his hair slicked down with bear grease, wearing a fringed leather jacket. He entertained people with romantic stories of the frontier. They called him "The American Woodsman."

An English critic said about his pictures: "In their motion and at rest, in their play and in their combats, singing, running, beating the air, skimming the waves . . . are real and palpable images of the new world."

French scientist Georges Cuvier said Audubon's paintings were "the greatest monument ever erected by art to nature."

Audubon raised enough money to begin publishing his *Birds of America*. Robert Havell Jr., a London engraver, agreed to engrave the 435 plates. The book was issued in four volumes between 1827 and 1838. A subscription cost $1,000 and he sold more than 200 sets. He also sold oil-painted copies of some of the drawings to drum up interest in his work and bring in extra money.

In 1829, Audubon returned to the United States, where he continued to travel and draw. He convinced Lucy to move to England. He and the family now had enough money to live comfortably. In the 1930s, he traveled back and forth from

Birds of America

Audubon's book, *Birds of America*, did not include all the birds in North America. It included 497 of the more than 700 species that had been identified on the continent. The first plate in the book showed the wild turkey.

The book was referred to as elephant folio because the pages were so large, measuring 39.37 inches high, over 3 inches taller than a yardstick. The pictures were engraved on copper plates and the birds appeared life-size on the pages.

All the printing was paid for from subscriptions, exhibitions, and oil paintings he sold. The actual cost of printing all volumes of the book was $115,640, which today would be over $2 million.

The last volume was issued in 1838. In 1840, Audubon decided to make a smaller edition, called an octavo edition. Philadelphia printer J. T. Bowen put out this edition between 1840 and 1844. Audubon added 65 plates to this edition. It was also sold by subscription.

Audubon's illustration of a summer tanager from *Birds of America*.
Library of Congress LC-USZC4-722

England to the United States several times. During this time, he finished writing the *Ornithological Biography* to go with the paintings in his book.

In 1939, the family returned to the United States for good. They bought an estate on the Hudson River in New York State. Audubon's next project was a book on mammals, called the *Viviparous Quadrupeds of North America*. He wrote the book with his good friend, John Bachman, whose

Audubon's tombstone in Manhattan, New York City.
Library of Congress
LC-DIG-ppmsca-23708

daughters were married to Audubon's sons. Bachman wrote much of the text. John Audubon did most of the drawings.

In 1848, Audubon began to show signs of old age and confusion. He died at his home on January 27, 1851.

Audubon had a great influence on both ornithology and natural history. His notes helped people to understand bird anatomy and behavior. His book is still considered a great example of book art.

Audubon was concerned about loss of bird habitat and the habit of overhunting. He was afraid some species would die out. Several birds in his book have become extinct, including the Carolina parakeet, the passenger pigeon, the Labrador Duck, and the great auk.

The National Audubon Society, begun in 1905, was named after him. George Bird Grinnel, one of the founders, chose this name because he had been tutored by Lucy and he knew Audubon had been interested in protecting birds and their habitats.

HENRY DAVID THOREAU
1817-1862

Henry David Thoreau is famous for his writings on nature and philosophy, and he was a forerunner of present-day environmentalists. But he never made much money, and he died at the age of 45.

Thoreau was born in a farmhouse in Concord, Massachusetts, on July 12, 1817. John and Cynthia Dunbar Thoreau named their baby David Henry, but he was always called Henry. Cynthia was a strong, outspoken woman, while John was gentle and quiet. The Thoreaus had two older children, Helen and John, and after Henry a younger girl, Sophia.

Young Henry's earliest memories were from the village of Chelmsford, where they moved when he was a year old. He recalled, "The cow came into the entry after pumpkins. I cut my toe and was knocked over by a hen with chickens."

Henry David Thoreau. *Library of Congress LC-USZ61-361*

Harvard University, where Thoreau earned his degree.
Library of Congress PAN US GEOG - Massachusetts no. 55

He also learned about God and that he would go to heaven when he died. He decided he didn't want to go there because he couldn't take his new sled. Another early memory was of lying in bed, looking out the window. He said he was "looking through the stars to see if I could see God behind them."

Henry idolized his older brother, John. He was funny and charming and had lots of friends. Henry was quiet, serious, and a good student. He loved being outdoors, running barefoot through the grass, fishing in the creek, and hunting. He soon gave up hunting and fishing, however, because he decided he didn't like killing.

He and John roamed the fields and woods, learning the names of the plants. They loved swimming in summer and ice-skating and sledding in winter.

When Thoreau was 16, he was ready to enter Harvard. His father's pencil business was doing well, so the family could afford to send him.

Helen used her teaching salary to help with his fees. Thoreau studied mathematics, classic literature, science, and rhetoric (English composition). He also studied languages, and by the time he left Harvard he could read Greek, Latin, French, Italian, Spanish, and German.

He loved the library and spent hours there every day. He was also able to continue studying nature during his college years and often wandered along the banks of the Charles River. There he found the home of an ermine, a furry white mammal, in the hollow of an apple tree. He visited it nearly every day that winter.

In December 1835, he took a term off to teach in Canton, Massachusetts. He taught a class of 70 pupils for six weeks. There he met Reverend Orestes Brownson, who introduced him to Transcendentalism. This philosophy opposed the strict rituals and narrow-minded beliefs of many religions. Transcendentalists saw a direct connection between the universe and a person's soul. They considered nature part of religion and thought people could discover the truth through awareness of the natural world around them.

While at Harvard, Thoreau discovered a book that changed his life. It was *Nature*, by Ralph Waldo Emerson. The book was a celebration of the wild, and it included concepts of Transcendentalism.

Thoreau was one of the high-ranking students of his class and was asked to speak at graduation in August 1837. In his speech, "The Commercial Spirit of Modern Times" he emphasized that a person should spend most of his time enjoying nature, not working.

Thoreau didn't think he had received a great education at Harvard. "What I learned at college was chiefly, I think, to express myself," he wrote later. He did learn to use the library, which served him the rest of his life. He also developed discipline, which helped him to carry on many of his own scientific studies of nature.

When he left college, Thoreau helped his dad make pencils for a while, then he got a job teaching in Concord. It was a good job, but he and the school committee had different ideas. He soon quit because he was told he had to use corporal punishment with the students, beating them or rapping their knuckles with a ruler.

About this time, he met Ralph Waldo Emerson, who was to have a great influence on his life. Thoreau was 20 and Emerson 34, but they quickly became close friends. Emerson encouraged Thoreau to keep a journal. On October 22, 1837, he made his first entry. He wrote that

someone had asked him, "Are you keeping a journal?" So he wrote, "I make my first entry."

Thoreau attended Transcendentalist discussions at Emerson's house and met many interesting people. He agreed with most of their philosophy, but later his beliefs became more scientific. He did believe in the Transcendental view that being close to nature helped a person to discover spiritual truth.

In June 1838, Henry and John Thoreau started a private school in their home. Some of the boys boarded with them. Bronson Alcott's daughters, Louisa May, Anna, and Beth were among their students. Students who couldn't afford tuition were allowed to attend for free.

Ralph Waldo Emerson.
Library of Congress
LC-DIG-pga-04133

Louisa May Alcott, **author of** *Little Women* **and** *Little Men*. *Library of Congress LC-USZ61-452*

JOURNAL LIKE THOREAU

Be like Thoreau—make a journal in which you can record your observations as you watch wild animals around you. You can watch animals in your own backyard or in a nearby park or wildlife area. You probably will see squirrels, rabbits, and many kinds of birds. Don't just write down the name of the animal. Watch it for a while and see how it acts and what it does. Write down how it looks and what it does. Look at Thoreau's journal entries about animals for ideas. Your journal will be more modern, though. It will be done on a computer!

WHAT YOU NEED

* Paper
* Pen or pencil
* Computer

WHAT YOU DO

1. Find a good place to watch animals, such as your yard or a park.

2. Take notes as you watch. Write what the animals are doing and how they look.

3. When you are through observing, type your notes into a file on the computer.

4. Keep adding to your journal as you continue to observe animals. Be sure to date each entry.

The school was quite different from others of its time. Henry wrote to a friend, "I could make education a pleasant thing both to the teacher and the scholar. . . . We should seek to be fellow-students with the pupil, and we should learn of, as well as with him, if we would be most helpful to him."

There was no physical punishment. John made it clear to the students that they must want to learn. He talked to students who broke the rules. Students enjoyed going into the woods and fields with Henry and learning about the animals and American Indians.

Henry taught natural history, science, and languages while John instructed the children in math and English. Once a week they took the students on a walk, a sail, or a swim.

In April 1841, John suddenly became ill and the brothers were forced to close the school. Soon after that, Emerson invited Henry Thoreau to live at his house in exchange for working as his handyman, companion, and babysitter. Emerson traveled a lot and felt comfortable leaving his wife, Lidian, and the children with Thoreau. The children liked him. Waldo, called Wallie, was five, and Ellen was two. Another child, Edith, was born a few months later.

Thoreau spent some of his time at the Emersons' home writing. He had published his first poem in 1840. He enjoyed life with the Emersons, but he was becoming restless. As he wrote in his journal on Christmas Eve, 1841, "I want to go soon and live away by the Pond, where I shall hear only the wind whispering among the reeds."

A few days later, John Thoreau cut his finger; within a week he had contracted tetanus, which causes the body to become rigid. His jaw stiffened, and he suffered terrible spasms. Henry went home to help, but even a doctor from Boston couldn't save John. He died in Henry's arms on January 11, 1842.

John's death was a horrible shock to Henry, and he never got over it. To make matters worse, little Wallie Emerson came down with a sore throat and fever on January 22 and died of scarlet fever six days later.

Thoreau had produced a lot of writing in the time he lived with the Emersons. Much of his

Emerson's home.
Library of Congress
LC-USZ62-132128

work appeared in *The Dial,* a transcendentalist magazine. He also helped Emerson edit the magazine. In May he wrote an essay titled "Natural History of Massachusetts." This was the beginning of his move toward becoming a naturalist, one who studies and interprets nature.

Thoreau was getting restless, and by this time he may have worn out his welcome at the Emersons'. Ralph Waldo Emerson got him a position tutoring the son of his brother William in Staten Island, New York. Emerson thought it would be easier for Thoreau to sell his writing to New York publishers if he were in the area.

But Thoreau hated life in the city. He wrote to Emerson that it was "a thousand times meaner than I could have imagined . . . the pigs in the street are the most respectable part of the population." He only managed to sell two pieces of writing while he was there. He wrote to his mother, "Methinks I should be content to sit at the back door in Concord, under the poplar tree, henceforth forever."

He did enjoy the ocean, though. He also met some people he liked, including Henry James, the philosopher, and Horace Greeley, the editor of the *New York Tribune,* who became a lifelong friend.

Thoreau arrived in New York in May and was home in Concord in time for Christmas. He lived with his parents and worked in the pencil business for a while. His writing

Horace Greeley.
Dover Publications, Inc.

career had stalled. His main publisher, *Dial,* had gone out of business.

In the fall of 1844, Thoreau helped his father build a new house for the family. This gave him some experience in building. He dug the basement and built the stone foundation walls. This was the first home the Thoreaus had ever owned, and they were very pleased with it.

Thoreau wanted to get away to a place where he could observe nature. Emerson provided the way. He bought 14 acres of land on the shore of Walden Pond and agreed to let Thoreau build a cabin in the woods near the pond.

Thoreau had wanted to live on Walden Pond since he was five years old. He was always trying to get closer to nature and simplify his life. At Walden he would be able to do both. He wrote, "I went to the woods because I wished to live deliberately, to front only the essential facts of life, and to see if I could not learn what it had to teach, and not, when I came to die, discover that I had not lived."

Thoreau was happier and healthier during his time at Walden Pond than at any other time of his life. If weather permitted, he bathed in the pond in the morning. Sometimes he worked in his bean field or hoed corn. In the afternoons, he went for long walks. In cold weather, he spent most mornings reading and writing.

Until he finished the fireplace, Thoreau cooked outside. He baked hoecakes (oatmeal cakes) and bread. He made a kind of molasses from pumpkins or beets but preferred maple syrup as a sweetener. He decided he did not need

(*left*) Site of Thoreau's cabin.
Library of Congress
LC-USZ62-39828

(*right*) Thoreau's cove at Walden Pond.
Library of Congress
LC-D4-34878

Building the Cabin at Walden Pond

Thoreau prepared his site beneath the pine trees and facing the pond. He wrote, "Near the end of March, 1845, I borrowed an axe and went down to the woods by Walden Pond, nearest to where I intended to build my house, and began to cut down some tall arrowy white pines, still in their youth, for timber."

He dug a cellar to store potatoes. He made the frame of the cabin with the pine trees. He needed boards for siding the house, so he bought a shack for $4.25. He tore the shanty apart carefully, saving all the nails to reuse.

Several of his friends helped with the house raising. Thoreau carried two cartloads of stones up from the pond in his arms. He used them to build the foundation for his fireplace.

He asserted his own independence by moving in on Independence Day, July 4, 1845. That summer and fall, he finished the cabin by building the chimney, fireplace, and stone hearth and plastering the walls. He spent $28.12½ on the materials.

He described his house this way: "I have thus a tightly shingled and plastered house, ten feet wide by fifteen feet long, and eight-feet posts, with a garret and a closet, a large window on each side, two trap doors, one door at the end, and a brick fireplace opposite."

His household goods consisted of a bed, a three-legged table, a desk, three chairs, a mirror, a pair of tongs, andirons to hold the logs in the fireplace, a kettle, a skillet, a frying pan, a dipper, a wash bowl, two knives and forks, three plates, one spoon, a cup, a jug for oil, a jug for molasses, and a lamp. He also had books, pen, and paper.

salt. He only ate meat when he ate with friends or family. He did eat fish and lots of vegetables, as well as wild berries, grapes, chestnuts, and hickory nuts.

Thoreau did a lot of writing at Walden. He finished a book, *A Week on the Concord and Merrimack Rivers*, which was about a trip he and John had taken. He also kept journals, as he knew he would want to write about his stay in the woods. He finished a complete draft of *Walden*, several lectures, and a third of his book *The Maine Woods*. He wrote a significant amount in two years, considering all the time he spent walking, observing nature, going into town, and entertaining company.

Thoreau thought a lot about the animals and the loss of their habitats. He wrote, "When I consider that the nobler animals have been exterminated here—the cougar, the panther, lynx, wolverine, wolf, bear, moose, deer, the beaver, the turkey, etc., etc.—I cannot but feel as if I lived in a tamed and as it were, emasculated [weakened] country."

He also was upset by farmers killing hawks to protect their chickens. "I would rather never taste

Common loon.
Dover Publications, Inc.

chickens' meat nor hens' eggs," he wrote, "than never to see a hawk sailing through the upper air again. This sight is worth incomparably more than a chicken soup or a boiled egg."

Thoreau took great interest in documenting everything he saw—signs of the changes of seasons, behavior of animals, and even the ice on the pond, which he measured and tested at intervals. He watched the colors change in the pond—green in the shallow places and blue in the deep. Many birds—chickadees, wood thrushes, brown thrashers, and martins—entertained him with their songs. He watched a fish hawk dive for fish and listened to the loons' wild call. On summer evenings, he often heard an owl hooting.

While at Walden, Thoreau became more interested in science. He found specimens of fish and other wildlife and shipped them to Louis Agassiz, a Swiss naturalist who had just come to America. Thoreau was able to provide specimens of two fish that Agassiz had never seen before.

Thoreau finally left the pond in late summer 1846, after spending a little more than two years there. He said he left the pond "for as good a

Red-tailed hawk.
Dover Publications, Inc.

Nature Observations from Thoreau's Journals

BARRED OWL

One afternoon I amused myself by watching a barred owl sitting on one of the lower dead limbs of a white pine, close to the trunk, in broad daylight, I standing within a rod of him. He could hear me when I moved and crunched the snow with my feet, but could not plainly see me. When I made most noise he would stretch out his neck, and erect his neck feathers, and open his eyes wide; but their lids soon fell again, and he began to nod.

Barred owl.
Dover Publications, Inc.

Fox.
Dover Publications, Inc.

FOX

I gained rapidly on the fox. . . . He took no step which was not beautiful . . . it was a sort of leopard canter, I should say, as if he were nowise impeded by the snow. . . . He ran as though there were not a bone in his back, occasionally dropping his muzzle to the snow . . . then tossing his head aloft when satisfied of his course. When he came to a declivity [a steep downward slope], he put his forefeet together and slid down it like cat. He trod so softly that you could not have heard it from any nearness.

Hare.
Dover Publications, Inc.

HARE

One evening one [hare] sat by my door two paces from me, at first trembling with fear, yet unwilling to move; a poor wee thing, lean and bony, with ragged ears, a sharp nose, scant tail and slender paws. I took a step and lo, away it scud [ran] with an elastic spring over the snow crust, straightening its body and its limbs into graceful length, and soon put the forest between me and itself.

reason as I went there. Perhaps it seemed to me that I had several more lives to live, and could not spend any more time for that one."

He wrote, "I learned this, at least, by my experiment; that if one advances confidently in the direction of his dreams, and endeavors to live the life which he has imagined, he will meet with a success unexpected in common hours."

Thoreau moved back in with the Emersons. Emerson went on a long trip to England and Thoreau was there to help Lidian with the children, Ellen, Edith, and little Eddy, who was born after Wallie had died.

During this time Thoreau sold some essays, and in 1848, he paid to have his first book published: *A Week on the Concord and Merrimack Rivers*. It got some good reviews but only sold 219 of the 1,000 copies he had had printed.

Although he no longer lived at Walden, he still spent much time enjoying nature. He wrote, "I cannot feel well in health and spirit without at least four hours a day sauntering through the woods and fields of Concord township."

Agassiz came to Concord and studied nature with Thoreau. A friend of Thoreau's shot a goshawk, and he sent the body to Agassiz. After

ANIMAL TRACK PLASTER CAST

Thoreau often found animals to observe by following their tracks. Here's how you can make a plaster cast of an animal track that you find in the mud.

WHAT YOU NEED

- Cardboard strip, 1½ inches high and long enough to fit around the track
- Paper clip
- Water
- Container to mix plaster
- Plaster of Paris
- Stick or old spoon to mix plaster
- Pancake turner

WHAT YOU DO

1. Find a good, clear animal track in the mud.

2. Bend the cardboard strip into a circle big enough to fit around the track.

3. Fasten the ends of the strip with the paper clip.

4. Press the cardboard strip into the mud all around the track.

5. Pour ½ cup of water into the container.

6. Pour in 1 cup of plaster and begin stirring immediately.

7. If your track is very large, use 2 cups of plaster and 1 cup of water.

8. Work quickly because the plaster will harden.

9. When the plaster is about as thick as pancake batter, carefully pour it into the track. Fill the cardboard mold to the rim.

10. Let your track set for an hour.

11. Carefully slide a pancake turner underneath the entire mold and lift it up.

12. Peel off the cardboard.

13. Let your track dry for several more days in the house. If there is any dried, caked-on mud on the cast, brush it off.

examining it, Agassiz determined that John James Audubon had been mistaken when he identified the goshawk as being part of the same family as the European falcon.

Thoreau enjoyed traveling and made several trips to the Maine woods and one to Cape Cod, where he was fascinated by the desolate expanse of sand and sea.

Thoreau's essay "Civil Disobedience" was published in 1849. He believed that if a law was unjust, citizens should refuse to obey it. He had once been jailed for refusing to pay his poll tax. His reason was that he didn't want his money to support either slavery or the Mexican War. Thoreau also worked against slavery, writing and delivering several lectures on the subject. His family once helped a runaway slave escape to Canada.

In March 1854, Thoreau found a publisher for *Walden*. He had self-published his first book, which means he paid all the expenses. This time the publisher, Ticknor and Fields, paid to publish the book. The first printed copy arrived on August 2. An announcement appeared in the *New York Tribune* and the book received several favorable reviews. However, it was not a big success, selling only about 2,000 copies in Thoreau's lifetime. He received a royalty check for $51.60.

In the spring of 1855, Thoreau became very ill. He had a bad cough and was so weak he could barely stand. He wasn't really well again until December. This was probably the beginning of his battle with tuberculosis, which plagued many members of his family.

Henry's father died in 1859. Now Henry was in charge of the family business and spent many hours filling orders for pencils and doing the paperwork his father had always done. He continued to lecture around the area.

Thoreau became more and more interested in science. He joined the Boston Society of Natural History and gave many lectures on nature. Thoreau was fascinated by forests and how they grow, including the way seeds are dispersed, or spread. He believed that seed-eating squirrels and birds were helpful to the forest, rather than destructive, as they helped disperse seeds. He began determining the ages of trees by counting the rings in the cross-sections of the trunks of felled trees. He discovered a cedar tree that had been alive before the Europeans settled New England in the early 1600s.

On December 3, 1860, Thoreau spent a cold wet day counting the rings of a tree. He became ill with bronchitis, a sickness of the lungs. He was sick all winter and was too weak to even write in his journal. Although he was strongly against slavery, he was too ill to even take much interest in the Civil War, which was just beginning.

His last trip, in the spring of 1861, was to Minnesota to study grassland plants and see how the American Indians lived. Seventeen-year-old Horace Mann Jr. went with him. He was the son of the great educator Horace Mann. When Thoreau returned home, his health was worse than ever. He tried to get back to making journal entries and sold some articles that fall.

People Influenced by Thoreau's Writings

JOHN BURROUGHS

The naturalist John Burroughs wrote about Thoreau in his first book, saying: "Time will enhance rather than lessen the value of his contributions. . . . Thoreau occupies a niche by himself, but Thoreau was not a great personality; far from it; yet his writings have a strong characteristic flavor . . . he has reference, also, to the highest truths. . . . Thoreau was, probably, the wildest civilized man this country has produced. Add to the shyness of the hermit and woodsman the wildness of the poet."

John Burroughs.
Dover Publications, Inc.

MOHANDAS GANDHI

Mohandas Gandhi, known for his nonviolent resistance in India, was deeply impressed when he read "Civil Disobedience." He said, "The essay seemed to me so convincing and truthful that I felt the need of knowing more of Thoreau."

Drawing of Mohandas Gandhi by Pogany.
Library of Congress LC-B2-5553-18

MARTIN LUTHER KING JR.

Another nonviolent leader, Martin Luther King Jr., gave Thoreau's "Civil Disobedience" credit for inspiring his civil rights campaigns in the south. His work was aimed at achieving equal treatment for African Americans.

By the beginning of 1862, it had become clear that Henry Thoreau was dying. He wrote in March, "If I were to live, I should have much to report on Natural History generally," but he added, "I suppose that I have not many months to live."

He had his bed brought downstairs so he could visit with family and friends, and his mother and Sophia took care of him. He was so weak the last month that he could barely whisper, but he was aware of what was going on. He died on the morning of May 6, 1862, with his mother, Sophia, and his Aunt Maria beside him.

Thoreau's writings have influenced many since his death. His books and articles are still read and enjoyed by many people today.

JOHN MUIR
1838-1914

John Muir came to the United States from Scotland. He attended the University of Wisconsin for a while, then set off on a walk across the country. He wrote more than 300 articles and 10 books about his travels and his philosophy of nature.

Muir was born in Dunbar, Scotland, on April 21, 1938. His parents, Daniel Muir and Ann Gilrye, had eight children. John and his next-younger brother, David, ran wild through the countryside. John later wrote, "I loved to wander in the fields to hear the birds sing, and along the seashore to gaze and wonder at the shells and seaweeds, eels and crabs in the pools among the rocks when the tide was low."

His earliest memories were of walks with his grandfather when he was about three. Grandfather also taught him the letters from shop signs across the street. John began school

John Muir. *Library of Congress LC-USZ62-7655*

at age three. He was very proud when he finished reading one book and could start another. His father made him memorize hymns and Bible verses and gave him a penny for learning "Rock of Ages."

At school the children learned to recite the New Testament. If they didn't learn their lessons, they were whipped. John's mother served the children oatmeal porridge in wooden bowls for breakfast. At noon they would run home, starving. Lunch was vegetable broth, a small piece of boiled mutton (sheep meat), and a scone.

After school, they had tea, a meal that consisted of a half slice of white bread, a scone, and warm water with a little milk and sugar in it. Their supper in the evening was a boiled potato and a piece of a scone.

John and the other boys collected birds' nests and eggs. Sometimes they took baby larks and kept them in cages, eventually setting them free. He said later, "Among our best games were running, jumping, wrestling, and scrambling."

He and David used to play a game they called scootchers after their mother put them to bed. A scootcher was a dare. Sometimes they dared each other to climb out the bedroom window onto the roof. Once David got scared and cried that he couldn't get back in. John grabbed him by the ankles and yanked him through the bedroom window.

When John was 11, he and David were with their grandparents when their father brought them surprising news. They were leaving for America the next day! Only Sarah, 13, John, 11 and David, 9, would be going with their father. The oldest sister, Margaret, stayed to help her mother with the youngest children, Daniel, Mary, and Anna. They would join the family after their father had built a house in America.

The Muirs settled in the backwoods of Wisconsin, carving a farm out of the wilderness. Life was full of hard work. They spent all the daylight hours clearing the forest, plowing with a team of oxen, and digging a well. There was no time for school in Wisconsin. They worked up to 16 hours a day in the hot summer, much of the time spent hoeing corn.

In winter, they got up at six o'clock, fed the horses and oxen, and brought in wood before breakfast. After they ate, they worked on fencing, chopping trees, and other tasks. If it rained hard or snowed, they worked in the barn. Here they threshed wheat, shelled corn, mended tools, made axe handles and ox yokes, and sprouted potatoes, which they stored in the cellar to be planted in the spring.

John began plowing at the age of 12, as soon as he was tall enough to see over the plow. He didn't sit on a tractor, as farmers do today when they plow. In John's time, an ox pulled the plow and the farmer walked behind and guided it. Until they could remove them, they had to plow around the stumps of the trees they had cut. Chopping up the stumps and digging them out was hard work. The only time John remembers not having to plow was when he had pneumonia and lay in the house for weeks, gasping for breath.

SCOTTISH OATMEAL SCONES

Make scones like John ate for tea as a boy.

WHAT YOU NEED

Adult supervision required

- ❧ Mixing bowl
- ❧ Big spoon
- ❧ 1¼ cups flour
- ❧ 2 teaspoons baking powder
- ❧ ½ teaspoon baking soda
- ❧ ½ teaspoon salt
- ❧ ½ cup brown sugar
- ❧ ½ cup (1 stick) cold butter
- ❧ Pastry blender or two table knives
- ❧ 1 cup quick-cooking oats
- ❧ ⅓ cup milk
- ❧ Cookie sheet
- ❧ 2 tablespoons melted butter
- ❧ 1 tablespoon granulated sugar (table sugar)
- ❧ Jam

WHAT YOU DO

1. Preheat the oven to 375 degrees.

2. In the mixing bowl, mix together the flour, baking powder, baking soda, and salt.

3. Add the brown sugar and mix in.

4. Cut the cold butter into small pieces. Use a pastry blender or two knives to mix it into the dough till it looks like coarse crumbs.

5. Mix in the oats.

6. Add milk and mix just until the dry ingredients are moistened.

7. Put flour on your hands and knead the ball of dough five or six times. Use enough flour so the dough isn't sticky.

8. On the cookie sheet, flatten the dough into a circle about 7 inches in diameter.

9. Brush the top with melted butter and sprinkle with granulated sugar.

10. Cut it into eight pie-shaped wedges.

11. Bake for 15 minutes or until the scones are lightly browned.

12. Eat with jam.

An ox pulling a plow.
Library of Congress
LC-58-12855

to myself,' I said. 'Five huge, solid hours!' I can hardly think of any other event of my life, any discovery I ever made that gave birth to joy so . . . glorious as the possession of these five frosty hours."

Besides reading, he used some of this new-found time to work on inventions. He invented a thermometer that could react to the body heat of a person standing four feet away. He also invented what he called his "early-rising machine." It was an alarm clock that would tip his bed up and dump him on the floor!

Muir's neighbors were impressed by the inventions. When Muir was 19, one of them suggested he take them to the Wisconsin State Fair. So the young man set off for Madison on the train, carrying several of his inventions. The engineer let him ride in the engine and watch how the machinery worked.

He started to buy a ticket to the fair, but when the agent found out he had something to exhibit, he said, "Oh, you don't need a ticket—come right in!" Muir went to the Fine Arts Hall, where the doorman was very interested in his work. He had brought two clocks and a thermometer.

"Did you make these?" asked the man. "They look wonderfully beautiful and novel, and must, I think, prove the most interesting feature of our fair." The man told him to place them anywhere he liked, even if he had to move other exhibits. Thinking back, Muir said, "They seemed to attract more attention than anything else in the hall. I got lots of praise from the crowd and the newspaper reporters."

The Muirs did have some good times, though. Their father had promised to buy the boys a pony when they got to America, and he kept that promise. Jack was a little Indian pony that Mr. Muir bought for $13. He was wild and threw John and David the first few times they tried to ride him. Within a month, though, they were riding him bareback with no halter or bridle.

John loved to read and wanted to stay up and read after the rest of the family went to bed. His father wouldn't allow that, but he finally gave John permission to get up as early as he wanted. John began rising at one o'clock. He said, "I had gained five hours, almost half a day! 'Five hours

Muir worked a few months in a foundry and machine shop, then decided he wanted to go to college. He enrolled at the University of Wisconsin, which he attended for several years. He worked various jobs to pay for his education. Muir didn't follow the regular course of study, but took whatever classes he thought would help him.

Muir never graduated. When he was ready, he moved on. He later said, "I was leaving one University for another, the Wisconsin University for the University of the Wilderness."

Muir worked in a shop in Indianapolis for most of 1866 and 1867. While adjusting a machine with a file, his hand slipped. The point of the file went right into his eye. He lost the sight in that eye, and soon the other one went dark, too. But after a few months, Muir's sight returned and he vowed he would spend the rest of his life enjoying the sights of nature.

He set off on a thousand-mile walk to Florida, where he came down with malaria. When he recovered, he sailed to Cuba, then to Panama. He crossed the isthmus, the narrow neck of land in Panama where the Panama Canal was later dug, then sailed up the west coast and arrived in California.

While in California, Muir asked someone for the way out of town. The man asked where he wanted to go, and he replied, "To any place that is wild." He ended up in the Yosemite Valley, where he spent much of the rest of his life.

During his first summer there, he worked as a shepherd, then he ran a sawmill near Yosemite Falls. In his spare time, Muir was always studying nature. He loved the Yosemite area, and wrote, "No temple made with hands can compare with Yosemite." He called it "the grandest of all special temples of Nature."

While studying nature, Muir came up with some theories about how the area had been developed. He became convinced that glaciers had sculpted the valley and surrounding area. At that time, most scientists believed that the valley had been formed by a catastrophic earthquake. But Louis Agassiz, a leading geologist of the day, agreed with Muir's theory.

For a while Muir worked as a guide, taking visitors around Yosemite. He was pleased when

Yosemite Valley.
Library of Congress
LC-USZ62-17948

his idol, Ralph Waldo Emerson, toured the area with him. Emerson tried to talk him into leaving Yosemite—he wanted Muir to teach the world what he had learned there.

Muir decided to stay in the mountains, working, learning. and writing. He finally left Yosemite in 1874 and spent some time in the San Francisco area. He lived with friends in Oakland for a few months while he wrote about Yosemite.

In 1873 and 1874, Muir studied the ecology and distribution of some of the groves of giant sequoias (redwood trees) in Yosemite. The American Association for the Advancement of Science published the paper he wrote describing his findings.

Muir Glacier in Alaska.
Library of Congress
LC-USZ62-61822

In 1874, Muir married Louisa Wanda Stentzel, known as Louie. Her parents owned a large ranch with orchards in Martinez, 35 miles from San Francisco. Muir spent the next several years successfully managing the 2,600 acres of vineyards and orchards. During that time, he and Louie had two daughters, Wanda and Helen.

John's health began to suffer from overwork, so Louie urged him to return to the hills and find his old self. He started traveling and climbed Mount Rainier. He wrote an article about his climb titled "Ascent of Mount Rainier." He also took several trips to Alaska. On his first trip there, he discovered Glacier Bay. He continued to travel and to write.

Muir had become convinced that livestock, especially domestic sheep, were a great threat to the Yosemite area. He took *Century* magazine editor Robert Underwood Johnson camping so he could see the damage caused by the sheep. Johnson offered to publish any article Muir wanted to write about the problem. He also used his influence to get a bill introduced in Congress to make the area into a national park. In 1890 Congress protected the area from grazing. Later that year, in large part due to the influence of Muir and Johnson, Congress created Yosemite National Park.

In 1892, Muir and some others created the Sierra Club. He said it was to "do something for wildness and make the mountains glad."

Muir's first book, *The Mountains of California,* was published in 1894. Two years later, he became friends with conservation leader Gifford

Pinchot. However, Pinchot issued a statement supporting sheep grazing in forest preserves. At that point, the friendship ended, with Muir saying, "I don't want anything more to do with you."

The conservation movement then split into two camps. The preservationists were led by Muir, while Pinchot led the conservationists. Pinchot believed in managing the nation's national resources for sustainable commercial use. Muir didn't believe in commercializing nature and thought the land should be preserved for its uplifting and spiritual values.

In 1899 Muir went with railroad executive E. H. Harriman on an exploratory voyage along the Alaska coast. They sailed on a luxurious 250-foot steamer called the *George W. Elder*. The two men became friends. Later Harriman put political pressure on Congress to pass conservation legislation.

In 1900, Sierra Club secretary Will Colby came up with the idea for a huge outing for the club. The next year 97 people, including Muir and his daughters Wanda and Helen, spent a month in Yosemite Valley. They hiked, climbed mountains, learned about the wilderness, and enjoyed campfire entertainment.

One woman who attended wrote, "Muir, the prince of mountain lovers, was guide and apostle, and his gentle, kindly face, genial blue eyes, and quaint, quiet observations on present and past Sierra conditions impressed us unforgettably with the 'sermons in stone, books in the running brooks,' he knows so well." The outing became an annual affair.

The Sierra Club

In May 1892, John Muir and Robert Underwood Johnson met with a group of people who were interested in promoting recreation in the Yosemite region. They established the Sierra Club with 182 charter members. Muir was elected president and held the office till his death in 1914.

The club's first project was to fight a proposal to make Yosemite National Park smaller. Throughout the years, the Sierra Club has dedicated itself to exploring and preserving American wildlife and wilderness. It is a nonprofit conservation and outdoors organization.

The current goals of the Sierra Club are to (1) move beyond coal; (2) find clean energy solutions to rebuild and repower America; (3) promote green (environmentally friendly) cars, fuels, and transportation for the 21st century; (4) limit total greenhouse emissions; (5) create resilient habitats; and (6) safeguard communities.

To learn more about the Sierra Club, you can check out their website at www.sierraclub.org.

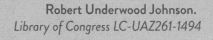

Robert Underwood Johnson.
Library of Congress LC-UAZ261-1494

A SQUARE YARD OF LAND

In this activity, you'll see how many plants and animals you can find in a square yard of land. If you have a big backyard, you can do it there. If not, go to a park or nature preserve.

WHAT YOU NEED

- ❧ Yardstick or tape measure
- ❧ 4 dowel rods or sturdy sticks, each about a foot long
- ❧ 5 yards of yarn
- ❧ Paper and pencil
- ❧ Camera (optional)
- ❧ Magnifying glass

WHAT YOU DO

1. Look around outdoors for an area that seems to have things growing (bugs, plants, etc.).

2. Measure out a square yard with your yardstick or tape measure and stick your dowels or sticks into the ground to form the corners.

3. Tie one end of the yarn to the first stick, near the top. Pull it to the next stick and wind it once around the stick. Go on to the next stick, then the last stick. Go back to the first stick and tie the yarn to it. Now you have a yarn square.

4. Get down on the ground and start exploring. List or describe the plants and animals you see. Draw a picture of each or take one with a camera. Use the magnifying glass to get a closer look. If there's a rock or small log in your area, turn it over. You may find some creatures hiding underneath.

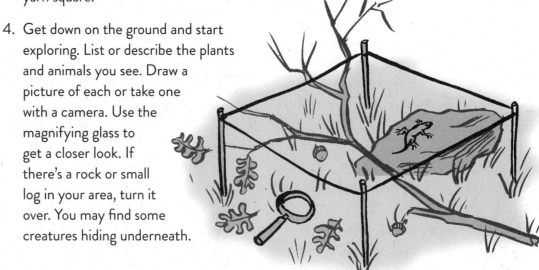

During his later years, Muir became more serious about his writing. In all, he published 300 articles and 10 books. He wrote about his travels and his philosophy of nature. He urged everyone to "climb mountains and get their good tidings." Readers were often moved by his enthusiasm for nature.

In 1901, Muir's *Our National Parks* was published. This book brought him to the attention of President Theodore Roosevelt. In 1903, Muir had a chance to meet Roosevelt and take him on a trip around Yosemite. He told the president about state mismanagement of the valley and how its resources were being exploited. They camped in the backcountry, talking late into the night. Roosevelt would never forget that trip. He was convinced that the best way to protect the area was through federal management and control.

Roosevelt fought many battles to protect Yosemite and the Sierra Nevada Mountains. In 1905, the Mariposa Grove and Yosemite Valley were added to the national park.

Muir's wife, Louie, died in 1905. John Muir continued his writing and conservation work. The city of San Francisco needed more water, so city officials proposed damming the Tuolumne River in Hetch Hetchy Valley to create a reservoir.

Muir, who thought the Hetch Hetchy Valley was even more beautiful than Yosemite Valley, was very opposed to the idea. The Sierra Club and Robert Underwood Johnson joined him in fighting against it. After years of debate,

John Muir and President Theodore Roosevelt.
Library of Congress
LC-USZ62-8672

Woodrow Wilson, who by then was president, signed the dam bill into law in 1913. Muir was crushed.

John Muir died of pneumonia in a Los Angeles hospital in 1914 at the age of 76. He had been in Los Angeles visiting his daughter Wanda.

Muir was perhaps this country's most influential and famous conservationist and naturalist. He is often called the "Father of Our National Park System." He was instrumental in the creation of Sequoia, Mount Rainier, Petrified Forest,

Yosemite, and Grand Canyon National Parks. He taught the people of the United States how important it is to experience and protect nature and the environment.

Muir Glacier in Alaska is named for him, as are the John Muir Wilderness, the Muir Woods National Monument, and many schools and parks. An image of John Muir with Half Dome and the California Condor was chosen to appear on the California state quarter, which was minted in 2005.

Muir's words and deeds have made people more aware of nature. He remains an inspiration for environmental activists today.

Theodore Roosevelt and the National Parks

Theodore Roosevelt was always interested in nature. After camping in Yosemite with John Muir, the president was convinced that federal control was the best option for protecting our most beautiful and interesting natural areas. He was instrumental in adding Yosemite Valley and the Mariposa Grove of giant sequoias to the already-existing Yosemite National Park.

Roosevelt said, "There can be nothing in the world more beautiful than the Yosemite, the groves of the giant sequoias . . . our people should see to it that they are preserved for their children and their children's children forever, with their majestic beauty all unmarred."

During his presidency, Roosevelt signed legislation to establish five national parks. They were Crater Lake in Oregon, Wind Cave in South Dakota, Sullys Hill in North Dakota (now a game preserve), Mesa Verde in Colorado, and Platt, in Oklahoma (now part of Chickasaw National Recreation area).

In 1906 Roosevelt signed the Antiquities Act. It gave the president the right to proclaim historic landmarks and structures as national monuments. Roosevelt named 19 areas as national monuments, including Devils Tower in Wyoming, Montezuma Castle in Arizona, and Petrified Forest, also in Arizona.

In recognition of Roosevelt's influence on the national park system, five areas have been named for him. These include the Theodore Roosevelt Birthplace National Historic Site in New York City, Sagamore Hill National Historic Site in Oyster Bay, New York, Theodore Roosevelt National Park in North Dakota, Theodore Roosevelt Inaugural National Historic Site in Buffalo, and Theodore Roosevelt Island in Washington, DC.

Roosevelt's preservation of many unique natural areas in the United States was one of his most significant contributions. National Geographic says, "The area of the United States placed under public protection by Theodore Roosevelt, as National Parks, National Forests, game and bird preserves, and other federal reservations, comes to a total of approximately 230,000,000 acres!"

CORDELIA STANWOOD
1865-1958

Cordelia Stanwood was a woman ahead of her time. In an era when women were given little recognition, she received acclaim for her thorough observations of birds. She was raised to be a lady and to pursue domestic activities. However, she turned out to be one of the "new women" in the changing world around her.

Cordelia, called Cordie, was born in Ellsworth, Maine, in 1865. Her father, Roswell Leland Stanwood, was a merchant sailing captain. Her mother, Margaret (Maggie) Susan Bown, was from a prominent family in Canada. They married in 1864. Until Cordie was almost eight years old, she, her mother, and her little sisters accompanied her father on his voyages.

Maggie didn't like life at sea and was often seasick. She was much happier when they returned to the house on Tinker's Hill in Ellsworth. Grandma Stanwood lived with them

Cordelia Stanwood as a young woman. *The Stanwood Wildlife Sanctuary* most of the time, and she taught Cordie about the family history and how to do needlework.

Cordie loved to roam the pastures, woods, and streams surrounding the house. One of her earliest memories was gathering strawberries and a mess of dandelion greens for Grandma Stanwood.

She remembered, "Another custom that my grandmother . . . had was to go out to spend the day with a friend. She would take me by the hand to walk with her to Mrs. Charles De Saittre's farm or Mrs. Lemuel Jordan's. I enjoyed going to Mrs. Jordan's particularly because she had a daughter, a young lady named Sarah, who would take me to walk in the woods."

She continued, "A roaring little stream ran through the Jordan land and poured into the Union River. Once there had been a mill over the brook. Some of the huge timbers still served as a footway across Card brook. The mosses in the woodland were numerous and luxuriant. Sarah would take a basket and we would gather a beautiful selection of mosses to arrange in deep plates when we returned home."

She also had pleasant memories of her father, and told this story:

At one time, Father owned a small sailboat. To our delight but to Mother's dismay, he offered to take us children and two of the neighboring children for a boat ride one day. As it happened, there was a brisk wind when we set out, and the boat skimmed over the waves gloriously. To my mother at home, this fine breeze seemed like a hurricane. Father caught several small fish and stopped at Shady Nook on the Union River to dress them. At a farmhouse he bought some milk, and after kindling a fine fire of driftwood, cooked a most delicious fish chowder. We famished youngsters felt sure we had never tasted so good a chowder before.

Cordie's grandmother taught her to read by showing her words for pictures of things she loved—trees, flowers, and animals. She also attended Ellsworth primary schools off and on.

When she was 14, her parents decided that she should go to Providence to live with her Aunt Cordelia, her father's sister, and her Uncle Oliver Johnson. Here she would be able to go to high school and be trained as a teacher.

On her arrival, she told Aunt Cordelia, "I have planned to earn my living by teaching." She lived with them and attended school for seven years. She took several botany courses in school. Her uncle often took her with him to his family farm in East Greenwich. She learned from him to be curious about the natural world.

Cordie graduated from Girl's English High School in 1886. She went back to Ellsworth to search for a job but was unable to find one, so she enrolled in a teacher training course in Providence. She enjoyed her year of training, but got a cold that hung on for weeks. Both the doctor and her aunt urged her to quit, but she said, "I have planned to earn my living by teaching and I can do no otherwise than to continue the course."

She got a teaching job when she finished. Wages were low, especially for women teachers. Most women planned to teach for only a few years until they found a husband. Married women were not allowed to teach. But Stanwood planned a career in teaching.

Teachers were expected to study during the summers to improve their teaching skills. For several years, Stanwood attended Martha's Vineyard Summer Institute. The two months at the seaside resort combined learning with rest and recreation by the sea. The school had a good reputation for teaching progressive methods and ideas. They had courses in nature study, photography, science, and the New Method of drawing.

Here Stanwood was able to enjoy a serious study of botany. She also learned new methods of teaching nature study and drawing. She made friends and many professional contacts. Professor Henry Turner Bailey taught some of the drawing courses, and he was to have a great influence on her. She corresponded with him for many years and became friends with his sisters.

She was also influenced by naturalist John Burroughs, who gave lectures and led hikes at one of the schools where she taught. She learned from him to write only what she observed and not to exaggerate or fictionalize.

After four years of teaching, even though Stanwood was primary principal of her school, she only made $700 a year, which was hardly enough to live on comfortably. Since art teachers earned higher salaries, she saved her money and took a course at the Massachusetts Normal Art

Lighthouse at Martha's Vineyard. *Library of Congress LG-DIG-highsm-12128*

School. This qualified her to teach drawing in the Massachusetts public schools. She taught art for several years.

In 1894, Stanwood became co-supervisor of art in the Springfield, Massachusetts, schools. However, she was dismissed from this job at spring vacation of her second year. Professor Bailey told his sister he knew of no other reason but jealousy.

Stanwood then served in Greenfield for a year as supervisor of art. Her job was to visit all the one-room schools to oversee the teaching of art. She had to learn to drive a horse and buggy in order to get from school to school. She only stayed a year because she couldn't face another winter of driving the buggy.

Stanwood identified her first bird while living in Greenfield. She remembered, "I heard my little friend, the black-throated green warbler for the

John Burroughs

Naturalist John Burroughs was important in the conservation movement in the United States. Born in 1837 on the family farm in the Catskill Mountains in New York, he became the most popular writer of nature essays since Thoreau.

As a boy, Burroughs was very interested in learning. His father didn't think higher education was necessary and refused to help him go to college. Burroughs got a job teaching and went to college part-time.

In 1857 he married Ursula North, a girl from back home. He sold his first essay to *Atlantic Monthly* in 1860. At first the editor thought he had plagiarized work from Ralph Waldo Emerson because their writing styles were so similar.

Burroughs became friends with writer Walt Whitman, who encouraged him to develop his nature writing. Some of his best essays were about his native Catskill Mountains.

Burroughs was friends with many famous people of the time, including Teddy Roosevelt and John Muir. He often traveled and camped with Henry Ford and Thomas Edison.

Most of his life Burroughs was lucky enough to have good physical and mental health. A few months before his death, he began having memory lapses. In February 1921, he had surgery to remove an abscess from his chest. His health went downhill after that, and he died the next month. He was buried on his 84th birthday.

John Burroughs.
Library of Congress LC-USZ62-130730

first time that day. It seemed to me wonderful that the lady [her friend] could hear that sweet strain in the tree . . . and recognize the musician without any effort."

Stanwood taught at several other places over the next few years. She taught drawing in the evenings to make enough money to live on and to send home to help her family.

In the fall of 1904, Stanwood resigned. She said she had a nervous breakdown and needed to rest, so she checked herself into the Adams Nervine Asylum, a mental health hospital that said it treated "nervous people who are not insane." When she left the hospital, she went back home. Doctors may have suggested she go to a secluded place where she could rest and recover. She planned to go back to teaching eventually, but never did.

Stanwood was living with her elderly parents and a young brother she barely knew, since he was born about the time she left home. She suffered from severe migraine headaches and depression throughout the winter. When spring came and she was able to get outside, she began to heal. She believed that being outside in nature kept her mentally healthy. She really didn't like being inside, doing domestic work, although she did help her mother with some of the housework.

By now, birds had become very important to Stanwood. "I never had time to study the birds until I stopped teaching," she said. She was determined to earn a living by writing about birds. She began her serious bird study, keeping field notes of birds she identified and their behavior. Her bird studies were based on the scientific method she had learned in her classes at Martha's Vineyard.

Not much was known about nesting behavior of birds, so Stanwood decided to make that her specialty. She was very good at finding nests and getting close to them. Early in her studies, she would take a baby bird out of the nest and take it to town to get photos made of it. Photographer Embert Osgood in Ellsworth photographed the birds for her. At that time, it was considered safe to remove the birds from the nests as long as you put them back. In 1912, Stanwood got her own camera. Now she could photograph the birds right in the nest. She sometimes still took the babies out and posed them on a branch to take their pictures.

It was not easy to photograph birds in the nest. Stanwood had to have enough light on her subject. She also had to put up with wind, rain, and mud. Sometimes she tied back branches that were in the way. Some of the nest sites were three miles from her house. And she had to carry heavy equipment while crossing streams.

When she went to the woods to observe birds, Stanwood wore a long skirt and high rubber boots. She often took neighborhood children with her to help carry her equipment. She enjoyed teaching them about the birds as they helped her.

Stanwood's family owned 40 acres, and she wandered three miles beyond it in all directions. She watched birds in pastures, woodlands, bogs, brooks, ponds, and rivers. She found out new facts about warblers, chickadees, woodpeckers,

(*left*) Cordelia's camera.
The Stanwood Wildlife Sanctuary

(*below*) Stanwood's photo of a mother bird feeding a baby.
The Stanwood Wildlife Sanctuary

and thrushes and reported them to other ornithologists, people who studied birds. Within five years she had become known for her extensive knowledge about birds. The community thought she was a little strange, but they proudly referred to her as Ellsworth's Famous Birdwoman.

Sometimes Stanwood built blinds (places to hide while observing birds) out of brush or canvas. She would sit there for many hours, observing the birds. It got hot in the summer and bugs crawled all over her, but she just caught them and saved them to feed to the baby birds!

Stanwood never developed her own photos because her house didn't have indoor plumbing or electricity. So she had to pay Embert Osgood to process them for her. Stanwood wanted to document the development of the baby birds by taking photos over a period of time at the nest. She always tried to get an artistic portrait of the birds.

She worried about the birds in bad weather. Stanwood once wrote, "I was out in Dyer Jordan's woods at the feet of a Redstart by 6:15. By 10 o'clock I was in the woods again, wet through. The rainstorm continued all that day, pouring violently in the afternoon and evening and all day Sunday. . . . I thought of the little mother Redstart, without even a leaf to cover her, sitting there with that heavy rain falling on her during the long, cold night."

Many magazines bought Stanwood's articles and photos of birds. Scientific magazines didn't pay a lot, but she was becoming well-known in the field of ornithology. The June 1910 issue of *The Auk* mentioned her in its "Bird Notes" column. Ora Willis Knight, a Maine ornithologist, wrote: "Recently I asked Miss Cordelia J. Stanwood . . . if she would not get careful measurements and a description of the bird for me, knowing she was a careful observer and bird

(*left*) Cordelia studying birds. *The Stanwood Wildlife Sanctuary*

(*right*) Red-breasted nuthatch.

WHAT DO YOUR LOCAL BIRDS EAT?

Learn what eight common birds in your area eat.

WHAT YOU NEED

- Bird guidebook or Internet access
- Pet supply store

WHAT YOU DO

First, use a bird guidebook or website to identify eight common birds in your area. Then make a list of typical foods these birds eat, foods that you can find or purchase. Birds vary greatly in the kinds of food they prefer. Although many birds like black oil sunflower seeds, there are many other preferences. Suet—hard fat mixed with seeds, nuts, and fruit—is the food of choice for woodpeckers and is also enjoyed by chickadees and nuthatches. The same birds love shelled peanuts. Blue jays like peanuts in the shell. Wild turkeys and quail like corn scattered on the ground. Niger seed is the food of choice for goldfinches, while orioles love orange halves.

Now see how many of these eight species you can attract to your yard by offering them the kind of food they like.

student. . . . In connection with Miss Stanwood's description and my own distant view of the bird I have no hesitation in pronouncing it a Whistling Swan, a bird new to Maine." It was unusual for a scientist to put that much trust in a woman's work at that time.

The Auk also noted that Stanwood had had articles published in a number of magazines. "Recent Bird Biographies by Miss Stanwood: numerous sketches of birds and their nesting activity have appeared during the last few years from the pen of Miss Stanwood, all of them evidently based upon careful study and written in a style that is pleasing and yet serious enough to suit the importance of many of the facts that are recorded." Stanwood published 20 of these nesting bird studies between 1910 and 1917.

Her friend Henry Turner Bailey read one of her articles and sent her this note: "My dear Miss Stanwood: I received the other day a copy of 'Nature and Culture' with your article on the red-breasted nuthatch. How well you do this sort

Egret.

Photo of Stanwood in later years. *The Stanwood Wildlife Sanctuary*

of thing! You stand a fair chance of becoming famous as a naturalist."

Besides writing about birds, Stanwood had articles published in teaching magazines. She also wove baskets and hooked and braided rugs to sell. In later years, she wrote educational and entertaining articles about birds for popular magazines. They also used her photos. These magazines paid more than the scientific journals, and she could sell the photos over and over to different magazines.

Stanwood was involved in politics at one time. She worked with her friend Fannie Eckstrom to get public support for a ban on selling feathers. Millions of birds were being killed for their feathers so women could use them to decorate hats.

Stanwood wrote a letter entitled "A Plea for the Birds" to the editor of the *Ellsworth American*. She described the horrors of hunting the white egrets for their feathers. Hunters would kill hundreds of adult birds, skin them, and leave the bodies to rot and their babies to die of starvation. Last-minute telegrams that Stanwood sent to legislators helped to sway them and the ban passed. Now she became known as a conservation activist as well as an expert ornithologist.

Stanwood continued to keep her notebooks until she was 88 years old. She donated her collection of photos to Acadia National Park, which is near her home. She gave her notes to the Ellsworth Bird Club. She fed birds in the yard at Birdsacre, her home, until she had to move to an assisted living facility when she was 90. Stanwood died at the age of 93.

Soon after Stanwood's death, a bird club member, Chandler Richmond, told the Rotary Club about her accomplishments. Rotary member Harvey Phillips, president of a local bank, was so impressed that he told Richmond he would back him if he bought Birdsacre. They restored the house and opened it as a bird sanctuary and museum.

If you visit Birdsacre, you can walk the paths that Stanwood walked while observing her nesting birds. You can go through the house and see the furniture that was there when she was alive. All her papers are also there.

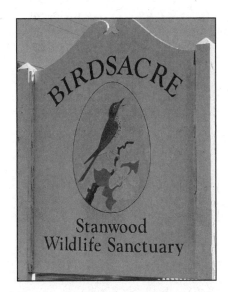

Sign at Birdsacre.

MAKE AN ORGANIC BIRD FEEDER

You can make a simple bird feeder that many birds will like.

WHAT YOU NEED

- ❀ Pine cones
- ❀ Butter knife
- ❀ Peanut butter
- ❀ Birdseed
- ❀ String

WHAT YOU DO

1. Use a butter knife to spread peanut butter on several pine cones.

2. Roll the pine cones in birdseed. The seeds will stick to the peanut butter.

3. Tie strings around the tops of the pine cones.

4. Hang them in your yard for the birds to enjoy. What species of birds do they attract?

Acadia National Park

Acadia National Park is located along the rugged coast of Maine, near Bar Harbor. It was the first national park east of the Mississippi River. Cadillac Mountain, the highest peak on the Atlantic Coast, is located within the park.

The park is a wonderful place for birdwatching, with 270 species breeding here. Small birds include warblers, chickadees, woodpeckers, and tanagers. Peregrine falcons and bald eagles nest on the cliffs. Along the ocean are gulls, gannets, and other seabirds.

You can also enjoy many other activities within the park, including climbing, fishing, hiking, swimming, picnicking, and boating. There are even activities just for kids.

Acadia National Park.
Library of Congress
LC-DIG-highsm

GIFFORD PINCHOT
1865-1946

Gifford Pinchot has been called the "Father of American Conservation" because of his great concern for protecting America's forests. He realized that our forests were not inexhaustible and believed in conservation of the forests by planned use and renewal.

Gifford was born at his family's summer home in Simsbury, Connecticut, on August 11, 1865. The family lived in New York City in the winter. His parents, James Pinchot and Mary Eno Pinchot, were wealthy. Gifford's father and grandfather had made a lot of money in the lumber business. However, his father had realized that clear-cutting forests caused problems. Clear-cutting means cutting down all the trees in an area, destroying the habitat and leaving the area open to erosion.

Gifford Pinchot. *Library of Congress LC-B2-1045-10*

James Pinchot taught his children to have an appreciation for nature and the forests. Besides the home in Connecticut, the Pinchots also had an estate in Milford, Pennsylvania, where Gifford spent a lot of time while growing up with his younger sister, Nettie, and his younger brother, Amos.

In the early 1870s, the whole family spent three years traveling around Europe. They visited England, France, Italy, and Germany. While at home, Gifford was a student at Phillips Exeter Academy in New Hampshire.

As Gifford was getting ready to enroll in college at Yale University, his dad asked him a question that might not seem strange now, but was at that time. He asked, "How would you like to be a forester?" It was strange because the United States had no school to train foresters and no forestry service.

Gifford later said, "I had no more conception of what it meant to be a forester than the man in the moon. . . . But at least a forester worked in the woods and with the woods—and I loved the woods and everything about them. . . . My father's suggestion settled the question in favor of forestry."

Pinchot spent four years at Yale getting a general education. Then he went to England to see how they handled their forests. He met Sir Dietrich Brandis, who was in charge of forestry projects in India. Brandis recommended he go to the National Forestry Academy in Nancy, France. He even wrote him a letter of introduction to the director. Pinchot was pleased to be going to school in France, since his family was French. He later wrote, "I presented my letters and was accepted as a foreign student by Director Puton on November 13, 1889—thirteen always was my lucky number—found rooms at the house of le Père et la Mère Babel, just outside the school gate, bought the necessary books, went to work, and cabled home for permission to stay, all in the order named."

Gifford took three courses at the school. First was silviculture, which he says "deals with trees and forests and what they are, how they grow, how they are protected, handled, harvested and produced."

The second was forest organization, which taught him about the economic side of forestry. He learned about all the money issues and "how

Campus of Yale University. *Library of Congress LC-DIG-ppmsca-18151*

to get out of the forest the most of whatever it is you want."

He didn't think his third course, forest law, would be helpful, since it was all about French law. However, when he eventually spent a great deal of time on US forest laws, he decided the course was more helpful than he had thought.

Gifford's favorite professor, Lucien Boppe, told him, "When you get home to America you must manage a forest and make it pay." Pinchot never forgot that advice. He returned to America in December 1890, but he still had to find a forest to manage.

He said, "When I came home, not a single acre of government, state, or private timberland was under systematic forest management." People believed there were enough forests to last forever, but Pinchot knew better. He decided there were two ways to go about changing that attitude.

One was to inform people of the need for forest management. The Forestry Association had already been doing that, with little success. The other way was to put forestry into practice in a forest to show that it was practical and could succeed. He chose this path.

Pinchot believed that forestry was tree farming. He said, "Forestry is handling trees so that one crop follows another. To grow trees as a crop is forestry." He knew that raising a crop of trees took much longer than raising a crop of corn or wheat. He realized that the person who planted the trees might not be around to see them mature.

General Sherman.
Library of Congress
LC-DIG-cwpbh-00593

During the next two weeks, he talked with many of the leaders of the forest movement in America. Then he spoke to a joint meeting of the American Forestry Association and the American Economic Association in Washington, DC. He read parts of his paper "Government Forestry Abroad."

Pinchot also met General William Tecumseh Sherman, who was interested in the environment. Sherman advised him to get to know his country better before he tried to put a forestry plan in practice. Pinchot took his advice and accepted a job from Phelps, Dodge and Company. He was to examine their forests in Pennsylvania and report on how forestry could be introduced

PLANT A TREE

Plant a tree in your yard. You can often get free trees to plant, especially around Arbor Day. Do a search online for free trees.

WHAT YOU NEED

Adult supervision required

- Seedling (small tree)
- Shovel
- Bucket of water
- Something to protect the tree after you plant it

WHAT YOU DO

1. Plant the tree as soon as you can after you get it.

2. With an adult's help, select a place to plant your tree. Make sure to locate it where it will have plenty of space to grow. Not only will it grow upward, the roots will spread under the ground. Be sure it's not too close to underground pipes or sidewalks.

3. Dig a hole deep enough to contain all the roots.

4. Place the tree in the hole with the root collar—the place where the roots meet the trunk—at soil level.

5. Pack soil around the tree, completely covering the roots and root collar.

6. Water the tree well.

7. Use something to protect your tree from people's feet, lawnmowers, and anything else thast might damage it. This could be a plastic jug with the top and bottom cut out, a small piece of fencing made for this purpose, or a series of rocks in a circle.

Child helping to plant a tree in 1920.
Library of Congress LC-DIG-npcc-18738

there. Since lumbering was such a big business in that area, he did not recommend the immediate introduction of forestry.

Soon after he finished that job, Dr. Bernhard Fernow invited Pinchot to go with him to examine some hardwood timber in eastern Arkansas. They spent 10 days there in the woods, then went on down the Mississippi River to New Orleans.

In the spring of 1891, Pinchot took another job with Phelps, Dodge and Company. This time he was to examine forests they owned in California and Arizona. It was his first trip to the far west, and he was impressed by the vastness of the land and sky.

Cornelius Vanderbilt hired Pinchot in January 1892 to manage his Biltmore Forest Estate near Asheville, North Carolina. Vanderbilt was interested in conservation. He also thought that a managed forest on the estate would be a good example to others. Pinchot improved the forest by selective thinning of trees. He also identified tree species and studied growth conditions, as well as determined the volume of timber per acre on the estate.

Pinchot put together an exhibit on scientific forest management for the World's Columbian Exhibition in Chicago. The exhibit included a pamphlet explaining his three main objectives: profitable production, nearly constant annual yield of timber, and improvement in the condition of the forest. His success at the Biltmore Estate was proof that forest management worked.

In 1897, Pinchot was appointed a special forest agent for the federal government. The next year

The Biltmore Estate.
Library of Congress
LC-DIG-csas-02190

Pinchot as a forester.
Library of Congress
LC-DIG-hec-04386

Reforestation

Reforestation is the restoring of a forest that has been reduced by either cutting or fire. It can be accomplished either by replanting or by natural regeneration. Replanting is done by humans. Natural regeneration is a gradual process where new trees grow from seeds or sprouts dropped by other trees in the forest.

Reforestation is necessary if humans are to have forests available for use by future generations. This is important for many reasons. From a monetary standpoint, timber is harvested and sold, making money for the owner of the land and for the loggers who work there. Without reforestation, the next generation would have no lumber to use.

Reforestation also helps to prevent erosion. When an area is clear cut, the trees and tree roots are not available to keep water from quickly running off the land, taking soil with it. Another benefit of reforestation is to provide habitat for wildlife, such as rabbits, deer, quail, elk, moose, ruffed grouse, and wild turkey. These animals live in areas where they can find food and shelter.

Forests also provide recreation opportunities. People enjoy hiking and camping in the forests. Birdwatching and hunting are other activities carried out in forests.

Reforestation is carried out by tree farmers and logging operations. Many different methods are used in reforestation. The method used depends on the type of trees in the forest and whether they grow best in shade or in sun.

Wildlife habitat is a driving force behind management which promotes recreation for the family to enjoy . . . forestry is a long-term investment with returns down the road. . . . It's important to pass on to the next generation. We view reforestation as a way to help the forest along, to promote species we want back, to select what grows well on different sites.
—Don Solin, Deerbrook, Wisconsin, tree farmer

As Gifford Pinchot emphasized, proper forest management will allow for profits as well as ensure an ongoing supply of forests to be used for logging and recreation and to provide wildlife habitat.

Reforestation project in Maryland.
Library of Congress
LC-DIG-fsac-1a34439

he was made head of the Division of Forestry of the Department of Agriculture. In 1899, the division was renamed the US Forest Service and took over control of the national forest preserves.

At that time Theodore Roosevelt was president, and he and Pinchot were friends. Roosevelt allowed Pinchot a lot of freedom to carry out his duties. Pinchot was dedicated to his job and worked hard. His enthusiasm spread to his staff.

Roosevelt and Pinchot have been credited with giving the name *conservation* to the movement for preservation and stewardship of natural resources. While Pinchot was in charge, the US Forest Service added millions of acres of national forests. In 1905, there were 60 national forests. By 1910 there were 150, and they covered 172 million acres. Pinchot controlled the use of the forests and managed their harvest.

Pinchot's philosophy was to do "the greatest good for the greatest number in the long run." He founded the Society of American Foresters in November 1900. He also founded the world's largest forest products laboratory, and he wrote conservation speeches for Roosevelt, who used them with very little change.

When William Howard Taft was elected president in 1909, he appointed Richard Ballinger as secretary of the interior. Taft didn't believe in government ownership of land. Pinchot accused Ballinger and Taft of not enforcing conservation policies. In 1910, Taft fired Pinchot and replaced him with Henry S. Graves.

Pinchot and Roosevelt.
National Archives

After he lost the forestry job, Pinchot helped Teddy Roosevelt organize the Bull Moose Party, which was a nickname for the Progressive Party. Roosevelt and many other Republicans were unhappy with Taft and thought he was doing little for the country. The Bull Moose Party supported the minimum wage, the right to vote for women, and worker's compensation. In 1912 Roosevelt ran for president against Taft and Democrat Woodrow Wilson, who was elected. Roosevelt got the highest percentage of the

SCAVENGER HUNT

Go on a scavenger hunt in the woods. You won't have to disturb anything in the environment, just keep a list. See how many of these things you can find.

WHAT YOU NEED

- ❖ Checklist
- ❖ Pen or pencil
- ❖ Camera

WHAT YOU DO

As you find each item, check it off on the list and take a photo of it.

ITEMS TO FIND

1. Acorn
2. Bird feather
3. Rock
4. Animal tracks
5. Insect
6. Flower (or berries if it's winter)
7. Fungus
8. Bird
9. Moss
10. Leaf
11. Evergreen tree
12. Deciduous tree (one that loses its leaves in fall)
13. Bird's nest
14. Pine cone
15. Squirrel

popular vote that any third-party candidate had ever received.

In 1914 Pinchot ran as the Progressive candidate for governor of Pennsylvania but was not elected. After that, he and Roosevelt both returned to the Republican Party. During the campaign, Pinchot married Cornelia Bryce, the daughter of a wealthy family. She worked hard as an activist for child labor reform, birth control, and women's suffrage (the right to vote). They had a son, Gifford Bryce Pinchot.

In 1920, Pinchot was appointed commissioner of forestry in Pennsylvania. As a forester, he established many of the state forests that still exist today. He also restructured the state forestry system.

Pinchot was still interested in becoming governor of Pennsylvania. He ran in 1922 and won. As governor, he was able to make the state government more efficient. He paid off the state debt and had a good record in labor-management dealings. Pinchot was controversial, though. Many people resented him for enforcing prohibition.

By law, Pinchot could not serve consecutive terms as governor, so he ran for the US Senate in 1926 and lost. He was re-elected governor in 1930 and had to face the challenges of the Great Depression. He created state jobs programs, especially jobs paving roads. Although he was a Republican, he supported President Franklin D. Roosevelt's federal aid programs. Pinchot was also among the first governors to include women, African Americans, and Jews in his administration.

After his term ended, Pinchot still fought for conservation causes in Washington. He developed

(*left*) Cornelia Pinchot and Gifford Jr.
Library of Congress
LC-DIG-npcc-22527

(*right*) Pinchot as governor of Pennsylvania.
Library of Congress
LC-DIG-npcc-14902

a fishing survival kit for naval personnel to use if they were adrift at sea. It was adopted by the US Army, Navy, and Coast Guard.

Pinchot also spent five years writing his autobiography, *Breaking New Ground*. The book was published after his death. He died of leukemia on October 4, 1946, at the age of 81.

Pinchot is known for being the first professionally trained forester in the United States.

He once said that he had been "a governor every now and then, but I am a forester all the time." He and Teddy Roosevelt are credited with establishing the conservation movement. Roosevelt said, "Among the many, many public officials who under my administration rendered literally invaluable service to the people of the United States, Gifford Pinchot on the whole stood first."

The Great Depression

The Great Depression in the United States began when the stock market crashed in October 1929. The stocks people owned were suddenly worth only a fraction of their former value. Thousands of people had invested all their money in stocks, and many lost it all.

The Depression continued throughout the 1930s. During this time many businesses failed and unemployment was widespread. Factories, stores, and banks closed. By 1932, a fourth of the American people were out of work. Many were homeless and had to depend on the government or charities to provide them with food.

Herbert Hoover was president when the stock market crashed. He believed the Depression was the result of a worldwide depression, and he thought the economy would have to recover naturally.

In 1932, Franklin Delano Roosevelt was elected president. Unlike Hoover, he believed there was a lot the government could do to help pull the country out of the Depression. His recovery program was known as the New Deal. In his inaugural address, he told the people of the United States, "The only thing we have to fear is fear itself."

Roosevelt didn't believe that he had all the answers to the problems of the Depression, but he was convinced that it was important to act quickly and try different methods to help the economy. He said, "Take a method and try it. If it fails, admit it frankly, and try another. But by all means, try something."

President Franklin D. Roosevelt.
Dover Publications, Inc.

Since unemployment was so high, one of the first priorities was to create jobs. Roosevelt formed the Civilian Conservation Corps (CCC). The program gave jobs to young men ages 19 to 25. They lived in work camps across the country and were paid $30 a month. The projects they worked on included planting trees, cleaning up stream pollution, and creating fish, game, and bird sanctuaries.

Members of the CCC (Civil Conservation Corps) at work.
Library of Congress LC-USF33-T01-000067-MI

The Civil Works Administration funded jobs for others. These workers repaired highways, dug ditches, and taught. Roosevelt favored programs that gave the unemployed work rather than welfare. Other programs targeted improvements to agriculture and industry.

Gifford Pinchot, although a Republican, backed the Democratic president in his programs. Pinchot himself found ways to provide many jobs for Pennsylvanians during the Depression. He was most proud of the fact that 20,000 miles of dirt roads were paved during his second term as governor, providing jobs for many.

ALDO LEOPOLD
1887-1948

Aldo Leopold's "land ethic" holds everyone responsible for protecting the environment. He wrote, "A land ethic, then, protects the existence of an ecological conscience, and this in turn reflects a conviction of individual responsibility for the health of the land." Leopold is well-known for his nature writing, which describes different environments and advocates conservation. His writings paved the way for the modern conservation movement.

Carl and Clara Starker Leopold named their new baby, born on January 11, 1887, Rand Aldo Leopold. He never used the name Rand. The family lived in a big house in Burlington, Iowa, atop limestone bluffs overlooking the Mississippi River. Aldo was the first child, followed by Maria, Carl, and Fred.

Aldo Leopold.

View from bluffs overlooking the Mississippi.
Library of Congress HAER IOWA, 29—BURL, 7—3

Carl Leopold owned a business that manufactured the finest quality walnut desks. He had a great interest in nature and used family picnics, hunting and fishing trips, and hikes in the woods to reveal the wonders of nature to his four children. Aldo was especially interested.

On fall mornings, Aldo and his dad would wake before dawn. They'd go to the railroad station for a breakfast of pork and beans and a baked apple. Then they'd take the train across the Mississippi. Crouching on a muskrat house, they'd listen in silence for the whistling sounds of ducks.

Carl was a duck hunter, but he refused to shoot any animal during the nesting season. At that time of year, he and Aldo would explore the marshes, discovering mink dens and figuring out what the mink had been eating. Carl's refusal to hunt during nesting season before it was made a law was a lesson in sportsmanship to Aldo. His father made that decision because he thought it was the right thing to do.

Aldo and his brother Carl were good buddies. They had an Irish terrier named Spud, and their dad had a hunting dog, Flick. The boys explored together, set traps, and had midnight snowball fights on the roof of their house.

Aldo spent hours exploring the woods, prairies, and rivers of Iowa. He loved observing nature, journaling, and sketching the things around him. He was a good artist and also liked to read. Aldo's brother Fred said, "As a boy, Aldo didn't talk a lot, but he was a smart student. He also read a great deal, especially books on wood lore. Even then he was becoming skillful at reading sign, knowing what the animals were eating, what had been chasing them, who was eating whom. He seemed to have gotten his love of outdoors from Dad." By the time he was 11, Aldo could identify all the birds he saw in the yard.

The family went on a trip out West in 1903, exploring the new national parks in the Rockies. Aldo wrote in his journal that he could think of "no better possible vocation" than forestry.

Muskrat.
Dover Publications, Inc.

Each summer the family went to the Les Chenaux Islands at the far end of Lake Huron. Six weeks in that climate helped ease Clara's severe hay fever. Aldo explored all of Marquette Island, where they stayed. He drew complicated maps of the island that showed the trees, animals, and landmarks, as well as all the trails.

One summer day, he found a skunk—his dad called them "sachet kitties"—and shot it. Imitating Daniel Boone, he carved on the boardwalk, "Aldo Leopold killed a skunk here on Aug. 20, 1901."

Dr. Simon McPherson from New Jersey lived on the island in the summer. He was the head of Lawrenceville Preparatory School and suggested Aldo go there. His mother was all for it, but Carl thought Burlington High School was fine. Aldo had started high school in Burlington. The school was so crowded, the students only had to go for recitations. Aldo loved this. He scheduled all his classes for the afternoon, leaving the mornings free to explore.

Aldo was a gifted student, but he was shy. His mother arranged for dancing lessons, but he didn't like them and remained a solitary person. In 1902 he began keeping detailed records of his bird observations. He went out early in the morning. Few people were out at that time, but he met Edwin Hunger, a poor newspaper boy. They became friends and birded together.

In 1904, Clara finally persuaded Carl that Aldo should go to Lawrenceville to school. He left on the train and arrived at the school five days before he turned 17. He liked the school, but he wrote to his father that "the instruction in English and History is much inferior to that of the high school." Aldo spent at least an hour a day tramping through the forests and wood. He drew maps labeled with names like Owl Woods, Ash Swamp, and Fern Woods. He wrote long letters home, describing his hikes and the birds he saw.

The school prepared Aldo well for college, and he entered Yale University in 1905. He still spent a lot of time in the woods, keeping observations of birds in a journal. In 1909 he graduated from Yale's School of Forestry. Gifford Pinchot had helped start the school, and Leopold was one of the first foresters to have formal training in the United States.

Leopold then joined the newly formed US Forest Service and was assigned to the Southwest. He

Skunk.
Dover Publications, Inc.

Duck hunters.
Library of Congress
LC-DIG-pga-01748

first went to Apache-Sitgreaves National Forest in Arizona, where he wanted to create a game refuge. The forest service turned down the idea, saying that wildlife protection was not part of their charter. He then went to New Mexico, where, at the age of 24, he was promoted to supervisor of Carson National Forest. He loved the area and often led crews into the mountains for surveys.

That same year he married Estella Bergere, daughter of a successful New Mexico ranching family. In 1913 Leopold became ill and had to be off work for nearly a year and a half.

When Leopold returned to work, he was assigned to the district office of grazing in Santa Fe. He was also asked to work on fish and game policies.

Leopold's interests were beginning to shift from forestry to game protection. He organized sportsmen in New Mexico and Arizona into cooperative game protection associations. He

Campers in Carson National Forest.
Library of Congress
LC-USF34-037165-D

also started a newsletter entitled *The Pine Cone*, the same name he had given his old newsletter in the Carson Forest. Leopold wrote a fish and game handbook listing the duties and powers of forest officers. He became interested in all aspects of the landscape in the Southwest, including erosion, game protection, and wilderness protection.

In 1918, Leopold left the US Forest Service to take a full-time job as secretary of the Albuquerque Chamber of Commerce. He saw it as a chance to continue working on game protection. He found time to write several articles, which were published. He wrote that he didn't believe people had to choose between civilization and wilderness.

In 1919, Leopold decided to return to the US Forest Service, taking the position of assistant district forester in charge of operations. This was the second-highest position in the Southwest district. He was responsible for 20 million acres of forest service land. Conservation of the land became his main concern, although he was still interested in game management.

Leopold was interested in setting aside areas within the national forests as wilderness areas. He submitted a proposal to have the Gila National Forest designated as a wilderness area, and in 1924, those 500,000 acres became the first wilderness area.

The same year, he was transferred to Madison, Wisconsin. There he served as assistant director of the US Forest Products Laboratory. Leopold was not very happy about being tied to

MAKE RECYCLED PAPER

Many materials today, including paper, are recycled in order to save natural resources. Recycling paper helps to save trees. Try making new paper from old.

WHAT YOU NEED

Adult supervision required

- Stapler and staples
- Piece of window screen at least 9 x 11 inches
- 8 x 10-inch wooden picture frame
- Old pieces of paper (computer paper, old envelopes, paper towels, tissue paper, etc.)
- Blender or food processor
- Water
- Sink or plastic tub big enough for the screen
- Colored threads, pressed flowers, leaves (optional)
- Old towels
- Hair dryer (optional)

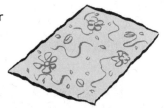

WHAT YOU DO

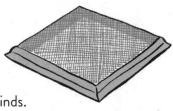

1. Staple the screen to the picture frame, making sure it's stretched tightly.

2. Choose paper to be recycled. You can use several different kinds.

3. Tear the paper into enough small pieces to fill the blender half full. Add water to fill the blender.

4. Run the blender, first on slow, then on a higher speed, till the pulp looks smooth and no chunks of paper remain.

5. Fill the sink or tub with a few inches of water. Put the screen in the water.

6. Pour the pulp onto the screen. Add threads, flowers, or any other material you want to use. Use your fingers to move the pulp around and flatten it so that it covers the whole screen.

7. Lift the screen very slowly and let the water drain out.

8. Put the screen on a covered flat surface. Gently use old towels to sop up the excess water.

9. Turn the screen over and scratch the back of the screen to loosen the paper.

10. Let the paper dry. You can use a hair dryer to dry it faster.

Leopold's Illness

Leopold went to a remote forest to settle a dispute between the US Forest Service and some sheepmen. It was a cold, rainy spring. His bedroll got soaked, but he had to sleep in it. The storm changed from hail, to sleet, to rain, to snow. He was on horseback and got lost taking a shortcut. His knees swelled, and he had to quit riding and take a stagecoach. A doctor diagnosed Leopold's problem as rheumatism. By the time Leopold got back to headquarters, his face, hands, arms, and legs were swollen.

He kept getting worse and went to a doctor in Santa Fe. This doctor told him he had acute nephritis and would have died if he hadn't come when he did. Leopold took a six-week leave from work. He was still in bed at the end of that time and the doctor recommended he go to Burlington to recuperate.

So a sick Aldo and a pregnant Estella boarded the train for Iowa, where they were welcomed by his parents. After three busy years as a forester, it was very hard for Aldo to sit on the porch day after day, looking out over the Mississippi River. When August came, he was allowed to go with the family to Les Cheneaux and do a little fishing.

In October, they returned to Burlington, where their first child, a son named Aldo Starker, was born. He was welcomed with joy as he was the first grandchild on both sides of the family. He was always called Starker.

Meanwhile, Leopold wanted to get back to work, but the doctors refused. He did some editing on *The Pine Cone*, a newsletter he had started. Finally, on September 14, 1914, he was reinstated by the Forest Service.

a desk or about leaving his beloved Southwest. The lab was mainly concerned with research on products to be made from the harvested trees. Leopold kept the job for four years.

In 1928 Leopold left the lab to do independent game surveys in the Midwest. In 1929 he gave a series of lectures on game management through the University of Wisconsin. He spent the next few years studying game around the area and writing.

In 1933 Leopold published a textbook called *Game Management*. That year, the University of Wisconsin created a department of game management and named him chairman. It was the first such department in the country. Leopold loved teaching and continued to do it until his death. His goal for the wildlife ecology course was "to teach the student to see the land, to understand what he sees, and enjoy what he understands."

In 1935 the Leopolds bought an old rundown farm on the Wisconsin River. The house had burned down, and the only building standing was a dilapidated chicken coop. By now, Aldo and Estella had five children, Starker, Luna, Nina, Fred, and Estella. The whole family worked together to restore the land.

They fixed up the chicken coop and named it the Shack. The family planted pine trees, prairie grasses, wildflowers, and other plants. Sometimes Leopold's students helped. Leopold kept records of everything they did and documented all the changes in the land. This was his way of putting

The Wilderness Society

The 76-year-old Wilderness Society works to protect our nation's 635 million acres of public lands. Their work has made great improvements in the way our national lands are managed and protected.

When the Wilderness Society was founded in 1935, Leopold believed it would spur the movement needed to save America's wilderness from vanishing. Today the society has more than 500,000 members and supporters. It has supported nearly all the major public land bills since its founding. The group helped to pass the Alaska National Interest Lands and Conservation Act of 1980 and the California Desert Protection Act of 1994. These two acts protected millions of acres of spectacular scenery in the Arctic and in the fragile deserts of the Southwest.

The Wilderness Society is still working to save the environment. During 2010 it supported 20 wilderness bills in Congress. However, the legislators took no action on the bills before adjourning. On the first day of the 112th Congress in January 2011, four congressmen introduced wilderness bills. The society is supporting them.

Late in 2010, Secretary of the Interior Ken Salazar ordered a new policy for protecting wilderness quality areas managed by the Bureau of Land Management.

The Wilderness Society continues to work on issues of global warming, energy, and unprotected wilderness. It works to persuade public officials, including the president and Congress, to create laws and policies that will conserve public lands. It also works to inform citizens of threats to conservation and try to move them to action.

University of Wisconsin.
Library of Congress
LC-USZ62-123458

The Land Ethic

In *A Sand County Almanac*, Leopold laid out the land ethic: "A thing is right when it tends to preserve the integrity, stability, and beauty of the biotic community. It is wrong when it tends to do otherwise." He also said, "A land ethic, then, reflects the existence of an ecological conscience, and this in return reflects a conviction of individual responsibility for the health of the land." He went on, "That land is to be loved and respected is an extension of ethics." In other words, he believed that all people have a responsibility to take care of the land.

his belief into action. He thought they could encourage people to practice conservation.

Also in 1935, he helped found the Wilderness Society. Leopold was asked to be president, but he didn't think he had time.

Leopold's experiences at the Shack inspired him to write a book of essays on conservation. In 1946, Oxford Press called to tell him they wanted to publish the book.

Sadly, he never saw the printed book. A week after that phone call, Leopold died of a heart attack while helping neighbors fight a grass fire that threatened the Shack. His son Luna oversaw the editing of the book, and it was published in 1947 with the title *A Sand County Almanac*. The book is best known for the land ethic it discussed.

A Sand County Almanac has influenced and inspired many people around the world. It has been printed in 10 languages and has sold over 2 million copies. It is one of the most respected environmental books ever written.

Leopold's home in New Mexico is now used by the US Forest Service. After his death, his five children formed the nonprofit Aldo Leopold Institute. Its goal is to teach people to care for the land and its creatures.

Called the Father of Wildlife Management, Leopold is largely responsible for the system employed in the United States to manage the wilderness. He is remembered for his nature writings, which paved the way for the modern conservation movement.

Paddling on the Wisconsin River.
Library of Congress LC-USZ62-65292

Aldo Leopold.
© CORBIS

MARJORY STONEMAN DOUGLAS
1890-1998

Marjory Stoneman Douglas is best known for her fight to save the Florida Everglades from development and draining. She was always outspoken about political issues, and people listened to her.

Marjory was born on April 7, 1890, in Minneapolis, Minnesota. She was the only child of Frank Stoneman and Lillian Trefethen, who was a concert violinist. One of Marjory's earliest memories was of sitting in her father's lap while he read to her from *Song of Hiawatha*. She remembered bursting into tears because the tree had to give up its life to provide Hiawatha with materials for his canoe.

She started reading at a young age and read constantly. Her first book was *Alice's Adventures in Wonderland*. She kept

Marjory Stoneman Douglas.

it for many years until, as she said, "Some fiend in human form must have borrowed it and not brought it back."

Marjory took her first trip to Florida when she was four. She and her parents went on a cruise from Tampa to Havana. She remembers picking an orange from a tree at the Tampa Bay Hotel where they stayed before the cruise.

When Marjory was six years old, her parents separated. She and her mother moved to Taunton, Massachusetts, where they lived with her grandparents and her aunt. Her mother's

Picking oranges.
Library of Congress
LC-DIG-ppmsca-18208

family was bitter about the split with Marjory's father, which made it hard for her. She described her mother as high-strung. Mrs. Stoneman was very nervous and very close to Marjory. She was hospitalized for nerve problems several times while Marjory was growing up. As she grew older, Marjory took on more responsibility in the family. Eventually she was managing some of the family's finances.

Marjory had lots of friends in high school, but she never dated. She wrote, "In ninth grade, we had cotillion dances. That's when I began to experience the awful ordeal of being a wallflower. I was fat, my hair was greasy, I wore glasses, I giggled, I was completely self-conscious with boys, and I wondered why none of them wanted to dance with me."

Marjory always enjoyed learning and already liked to write when she was in high school. She loved reading and doing research. Then graduation drew near. "I wanted to go to a good college," she remembered, "and my mind was set on Wellesley. Wellesley was the nearest good college in those days and I chose it even though my good friends were going elsewhere." One reason she wanted to go there was that it was a women's college.

Her family didn't have much money, but they always expected Marjory to go to college. Aunt Fanny paid many of her college expenses, having saved the money she made from giving music lessons for years.

Douglas knew it would be hard for her mother to be separated from her, but she also realized that it was important for her to get away. She quickly made many friends. Douglas majored in English composition. Since she had done so well in all her high school English courses, she was put in an advanced English class. Some of her writing was published in the college literary magazine, which made her feel like a real writer.

She enjoyed her class in elocution, which involved learning to pronounce words correctly. The professor helped the students to get rid of their various accents, insisting that they articulate their words in a specific way. In later years when she was making many speeches Douglas was very grateful she had taken this course.

When Douglas went home for Christmas during her junior year of college, her mother showed her a large lump in her breast. She had to have surgery to remove the cancer. Douglas was with her mother for her entire hospital stay. She spent spring vacation at home with her mother as she recuperated.

During her senior year, Douglas was very involved in school activities. She was named editor of the college yearbook, her first job in publishing. She played Friar Tuck in the senior play, which was *Sherwood Forest*. She was also thrilled to be elected class orator, but she couldn't accept because students were only allowed to participate in two major activities.

Douglas still didn't know what she wanted to do after graduation. Her grandmother wanted her to become a teacher so she could make a living, but she hated the idea.

Wellesley College. *Library of Congress LC-USZ62-124298*

Friar Tuck, second from left. *Library of Congress LC-DIG-ppmsca-26018*

Douglas's aunt and cousin came to her graduation, which made her very happy. However, after the ceremony, they told her they had some bad news. Her mother was dying of cancer of the spine. She was in great pain. A few hours after graduation, Douglas was at her mother's bedside.

When her mother died, Douglas made all the funeral arrangements and took care of all the details. Strangely, her mother's sister, Aunt Alice, who had come for the funeral, died while she was there. It was a sad summer.

A green heron in the Everglades.

Douglas and two friends signed up for a training program in Boston that would teach them to train salesgirls in department stores. After the training, she got a job in a department store in St. Louis where her best friend, Carolyn Percy, was teaching. She stayed for a year. When Percy moved back with her family, Douglas found a job in a department store in Newark, New Jersey. She didn't like Newark, and she didn't like the job.

About that time, she met Kenneth Douglas, the editor of a newspaper. He was about 30 years older than she was, but he began asking her out. She was so shocked to have a man pay so much attention to her that she married him after three months.

Things went well for a while, but then Kenneth was sentenced to six months in prison for forging a check. He told her he'd been framed and she stuck with him, visiting every Sunday.

After Kenneth had been out of prison for a while, without a job, her uncle visited her and explained that Kenneth had tried to get money from her father in Florida. Uncle Ned told Douglas that if she stayed with Kenneth, she would be implicated in the illegal things he was doing.

Douglas believed her uncle. He then told her that her father wanted her to come live with him and his new wife in Florida. He sent her money for the trip. Kenneth didn't seem upset when she told him she was leaving.

She was excited as the train took her closer and closer to Florida. She was a little nervous, though, since she hadn't seen her dad since she was six. She needn't have worried. He greeted her with a kiss, saying, "Hello, sweetheart." Her new stepmother, Lilla, welcomed her with a big hug and became her best friend.

Douglas's father was the editor of the newspaper that later became the *Miami Herald*. The society editor quit, so Mr. Stoneman gave Douglas the job. She was a little bored, reporting on parties, teas, and weddings. There wasn't a lot of news in the little town, so she sometimes made up things. She said, "Somebody would say, 'Who's that Mrs. T. Y. Washrag you've got in your column?' And I would say, 'Oh, you know, I don't think she's been here very long!'"

It was about this time that Douglas first heard about the Everglades. The governor of Florida, Napoleon Bonaparte Broward, was determined to drain this area of wetlands. Douglas's father wrote many articles against the idea. The governor was so upset with him that when Stoneman was elected judge, Broward never validated the election. From that time on, though, people called Stoneman "Judge."

When Stoneman went on a trip, he put Douglas in charge of the editorial page. She developed a rivalry with a reporter on the *Miami Metropolis*. The woman was more familiar with Miami history and sometimes made fun of the things Douglas wrote. Her father told her she needed to check her facts.

She was soon writing hard-hitting editorials on controversial subjects. She wrote about women's rights, racial justice, and conservation. She wrote of the need to protect Florida's

Red Cross poster.
Library of Congress
LC-USZC4-10138

natural resources from the rapid commercial development.

In 1916, during World War I, Douglas's father assigned her to cover the first woman joining the US Naval Reserve from Miami. When the woman didn't show up, she joined the reserve herself, in order to have a story! But she was bored, so she asked for a discharge and joined the American Red Cross. She was sent to Paris, where she cared for war refugees. She later

The Everglades

For many years, the Everglades were considered a useless swamp that needed to be drained. However, the area is not a swamp at all, but a very shallow, ever-moving river filled with sawgrass. It plays an important role in Florida's weather and climate. Marjory Stoneman Douglas wrote,

Much of the rainfall on which Southern Florida depends comes from evaporation in the Everglades. The Everglades evaporate, the moisture goes up into the clouds, the clouds are blown to the north, and the rain comes down over the Kissimmee River and Lake Okeechobee. Lake Okeechobee, especially, is fed by these rains. When the lake gets filled, some of the excess drains down the Cahoosahatchee River into the Gulf of Mexico, or through the St. Lucie River and into the Atlantic Ocean. The rest of the excess, the most useful part, spills over the southern rim of the lake into the great arc of the Everglades.

After that happens, the water moves slowly but steadily southward. Douglas was right when she wrote that there was nowhere else in the world like the Everglades. It's a unique ecosystem.

Great blue heron.

said that seeing those people in a state of shock "helped me understand the plight of refugees in Miami sixty years later."

When Douglas returned home, she was promoted to assistant editor of the paper and began writing a daily column called "The Galley." She became a local celebrity. She also wrote ad copy for extra money, and she wrote short stories in her spare time.

Douglas was concerned about the plight of the black people in the Miami area. Each city had a section called "Colored Town," where the black residents lived. The Colored Town in Miami had no toilets and no running water. People got sick from the polluted water caused by sewage running into the well.

Douglas and some friends managed to get a law passed that every house had to have a toilet and a bathtub. They set up a loan program where black residents could borrow money to install plumbing. They didn't have to pay interest, and she noted that every loan was paid back. She also set up a baby milk fund through the newspaper. People donated money to provide milk for young children.

In 1924 Douglas began suffering from nervous fatigue. She was under a lot of pressure at the newspaper and was having trouble sleeping. She finally had a nervous breakdown and had to take time off. She did a lot of writing while she was recovering and sold several of her short stories. That summer, she used the money she'd saved to go to Taunton to visit her grandmother and her aunt. She began selling stories to the *Saturday Evening Post.* She was making enough money selling her writing that she was able to quit the newspaper. She wrote many stories with a Florida setting, and some had conservation themes.

Douglas decided to move out of her father's home. So at age 34, she built a house in nearby Coconut Grove. The house was finished in the fall of 1926. It mostly consisted of one big room, with a small kitchenette and a bedroom. It had no air conditioning, but it was built to take advantage of the breezes. She never had a stove; she cooked on a hot plate.

In the early 1940s, editor Harvey Allen asked Douglas to write a book on the Miami River for his Rivers of America series. She laughed, saying, "Harvey, you can't write a book about the Miami River. It's only about an inch long." However, she talked him into letting her write a book on the Everglades instead. She said it took her four or five years to do all the research. She called it "an idea that would consume me for the rest of my life."

The book, *The Everglades: River of Grass,* came out in 1947. Before its publication, people had thought of the Everglades as a useless swamp that needed to be drained. Douglas's book showed them it was a valuable part of Florida's environment that needed to be protected. The book begins, "There are no other Everglades in the world. They are, they always have been one of the unique regions of the earth; remote, never

wholly known. Nothing anywhere else is like them."

The Everglades book had as much impact as Rachel Carson's book, *Silent Spring,* would have when it was published in 1962. Both books called attention to the environment and the need to protect and preserve it. *Christian Science Monitor* wrote of Douglas's book in 1997, "Today her book is not only a classic of environmental literature, it also reads like a blueprint for what conservationists are hailing as the most extensive environmental restoration project ever undertaken anywhere in the world."

The same year the book came out, President Harry S. Truman designated the Everglades a national park. Much of the credit is due to Douglas's hard work.

When the book started making money, Douglas took her first trip out West. She and two friends went to New Orleans, San Antonio, El Paso, Phoenix, and Los Angeles. She visited her father's sister, her aunt Stella, in Claremont, California. They visited the Grand Canyon on the way back.

When Douglas got back to Florida, she finished the novel she'd been working on and was able to sell it to a publisher. It didn't sell nearly as well as the Everglades book. Next she wrote a book about a Quaker boy, a Miccosukee Indian boy, and an escaped slave. The book, *Freedom River,* sold fairly well. In the mid-1950s, the company that had published *The Everglades: River of Grass* asked Marjory to write a book on

ALLIGATORS AND CROCODILES

Both alligators and crocodiles live in the Everglades, but alligators are much more common. The two look similar, but there are several differences. Here's how to make a poster that will show people the differences.

WHAT YOU NEED

❖ Poster board

❖ Markers or crayons

❖ Computer with online access

WHAT YOU DO

1. Divide your poster board into two halves. Label one side "Alligators" and the other side "Crocodiles."

2. Research alligators and crocodiles online and find at least three differences. For example, their snouts are different shapes. So on one side of the poster, draw an alligator snout, and on the other side draw a crocodile snout. Find two other differences that you can illustrate.

3. Draw and color your pictures.

Alligator in Florida.

hurricanes. She traveled a lot, gathering information and interviewing people who had been through hurricanes, from Miami to Cuba to Jamaica. The book was published in 1958 and sold well. She continued writing and lecturing through the 1960s.

When she was 78 years old, Douglas got involved with the Everglades again. First she helped fight a plan to put an oil refinery on Biscayne Bay. As soon as that idea was killed, someone came up with the idea of building a big airport in the Everglades. There was already a small landing strip for private planes, and it was stopping the flow of the water. The airport would cause much more damage.

To help with her fight, Douglas started an organization called Friends of the Everglades. She went around making speeches to any organization that would listen. The jetport idea was finally defeated. The Friends of the Everglades now has about 4,000 members.

Douglas was a tiny lady, five feet two inches tall and barely 100 pounds. She always wore a dress, pearls, a floppy straw hat, and gloves. She wrote, "People can't be rude to me—this poor little old woman. But I can be rude to them, poor darlings, and nobody can stop me." Another time she said, "I take advantage of everything I can—age, hair, disability—because my cause is just."

When she was in her late 90s, Douglas wrote, "Since 1972, I've been going around making speeches on the Everglades all over the place. No matter how poor my eyes are I can still talk. I'll talk about the Everglades at the drop of a hat. . . .

Marjory Stoneman Douglas examines a grass stalk in the Everglades, 1989.
© Kevin Fleming/CORBIS

Sometimes, I tell them more than they wanted to know."

Douglas was also concerned about the wildlife in the Everglades. She was an animal lover and always had cats at home. The Florida panther was in danger of extinction, so the government decided to catch all the panthers and put collars on them so they could trace where they were. Douglas hated that idea. She knew cats didn't like collars. She was afraid the collars would get caught on tree limbs and the cats could be strangled. This was one fight she didn't win.

Most of Douglas's last 30 years were spent traveling around, speaking to groups about the Everglades. She once said, "The Everglades is a test—if we pass it, we may get to keep the planet."

Florida panther.
Dover Publications, Inc.

The Florida Panther

The Florida panther now lives only in a small area of the state. Its range used to include parts of eight southeastern states. The area where the panthers now live includes Big Cypress National Preserve, Corkscrew Swamp, and the Everglades National Park.

The Florida panther is a large, tan cat with black markings on the tip of the tail, the ears, and around the nose. The adult is six to seven feet long. Adult panthers are loners. They don't associate with other adult panthers except to mate. Females have one to three kittens at a time. Only about half of those kittens live until their first birthday, and half of those don't live to be two years old. The kittens only weigh a pound and are spotted, to help camouflage them. They stay with their mother for a year or two.

Life is dangerous for baby panthers. They can be eaten by alligators, wild pigs, or birds of prey. The adults eat meat, including birds, wild pigs, and white-tailed deer. The average life span for a panther that makes it to adulthood is 12 years. Some live to be 20.

Some panthers are killed by cars. You're very unlikely to see a panther in the wild, as they are very shy. They usually travel at night.

An adult panther needs a large territory in which to hunt. Adult panthers are territorial and won't share an area with another panther. At times, one panther kills another over territory. Loss of habitat is a big problem for the panthers. Much of Florida land has been made into farms, housing developments, and shopping centers. This leaves less land for the panther to roam.

Steps are being taken to cut down on deaths from automobiles. In many areas, chain-link fences prevent the panthers from crossing highways. One area plans to try a system that will detect a panther in the area and warn motorists. Others are trying to set aside more preserves for the animals.

A few years ago, fewer than 100 of the big cats remained in Florida. In 2009, scientists counted 113. The panther has been on the endangered animal list since 1973.

Marjory received many awards. In 1993, President Bill Clinton awarded her the Presidential Medal of Freedom. This is the highest honor that can be given to a civilian. In 2000, she made the National Women's Hall of Fame. When she heard she was being considered for that, she asked, "Why should they have a Women's Hall of Fame? . . . Why not a Citizen's Hall of Fame?" Some awards came after she died. The year after her death, she was inducted into the National Wildlife Federation Hall of Fame.

On May 14, 1998, Marjory Stoneman Douglas passed away at the age of 108. John Rothchild, who had helped her write her autobiography, said death was the only thing that could "shut her up," but noted, "The silence is terrible."

Douglas's life shows what one person can accomplish if she puts her mind to it and doesn't give up. She spent 50 years convincing people of the importance of saving the Everglades. She had greater influence in this area than anyone before or since.

President Bill Clinton.
Library of Congress
LC-USZ62-107700

MARGARET "MARDY" MURIE
1902-2003

Margaret "Mardy" Murie.

Mardy Murie and her husband, Olaus, helped to establish Grand Teton National Park in Wyoming. They also worked hard to get land set aside in Alaska for the Arctic National Wildlife Refuge. Mardy lived for 40 years after Olaus died. Right to the end, she carried on with the work they had started together. Both the Sierra Club and the Wilderness Society referred to her as the "Grandmother of the Conservation Movement."

Margaret Elizabeth Thomas was born in Seattle, Washington, on August 18, 1902. She was always known as Mardy. Soon after her birth, her parents, Minnie and Ashton Thomas, moved to Juneau, Alaska. When she was five, her parents divorced and Mardy and her mother moved to Seattle. There

Mardy Murie.
The Murie Center

come up with her apron full of fish!" Besides playing outside, Mardy loved babysitting for the Rust children next door.

Mardy went to Reed College in Oregon. Her parents hoped she would become a secretary. After two years at Reed, she transferred to Simmons College in Boston. She spent her last year of college at the University of Alaska, then known as the Agricultural College and School of Mines. She graduated with a business degree and was the first woman to graduate from the school.

A couple of years earlier, the Rust family next door had introduced her to Olaus Murie. He worked for the Biological Survey, which later became the US Fish and Game Service. Their son Donald later said, "She found my father mysterious and it took awhile for her to understand him."

Mardy recalled, "We walked home together in the rosy northern evening; all I remember is that we agreed we didn't care to live in cities. He didn't say, 'When may I see you again?' as all the rest of them did. He was not like any of the rest of them, and it took me quite awhile to understand this."

Soon after her graduation, Mardy and Olaus were married in a 3:00 AM sunrise service in the Alaskan village of Anvik. Their honeymoon was spent studying Alaska caribou along the Koyukuk River. They traveled by dogsled and boat.

Mardy loved her new life and pitched in to help with the research. She wrote, "An ideal day to hit the trail: 12 below, just right for mushing. We were both running, and I was soon too warm; I threw back the parka hood and pulled

her mother met and married Louis R. Gillette. He worked in Fairbanks, Alaska. Gillette was assistant US attorney for the territory of Alaska, which was not yet a state.

When Mardy was nine, her stepfather sent for her and her mother to join him. They had just three days to catch the last steamer of the season. Once the rivers froze up, all travel would be delayed until spring. The trip took three weeks. The family rented a small four-room house at the edge of Fairbanks. Mardy's half-sister Louise was born soon after they moved to Alaska.

Mardy loved Alaska. She wrote later that she thrived on the "wild, free, clean, fragrant, untrampled" nature of the land. Her stepfather recalled, "Why, if she fell in the creek, Mardy'd off the red toque [hat]; the crisp air felt good on my bared head. How light my moccasined feet felt, padding along on the snow-sprinkled ice at a dogtrot, exhilaration in every muscle responding to the joy of motion, running, running without getting out of breath."

Mardy quickly adapted to being a wife instead of a college girl. "I did not try to put my hair into its usual Elsie Ferguson puffed and rolled style," she wrote. "I parted it in the middle and combed it into two long braids to hang over my shoulders; this was the way it would have to be for the coming months."

In 1926 she and Olaus took their 10-month-old baby, Martin, with them on a trip to band geese and study caribou. They strapped a wooden box in the boat. Here, Mardy said, "he sat, or jumped up and down, or slept, clad in khaki coveralls." A baby harness held him in the boat. "The boat was open, and the rushing relentless water was right there beside us," she continued.

Olaus had missed Martin's birth. From that time on, Mardy went everywhere with him. As the other children, Joanne and Donald, came along, they were also included in expeditions. The Muries worked in the Arctic till 1927. They studied and documented the birds, vegetation, mammals, habitats, and topography of the area.

In 1927 Olaus was sent to Wyoming to study the elk herd in Jackson Hole, which seemed to be declining. They built a log cabin at the foot of the Teton Mountains. In the summer, the whole family spent months camping wherever Olaus was working.

According to Mardy, "Camp life suited me; it was naturally no trouble for me to settle into it. Many women have asked me, 'How did you manage the children way off there in the hills?' Well, all I can say is that it was simpler there than in town. They were well fed, and because they were busy in the open air every moment, their appetites were wonderful; they grew and were brown and never had a sick moment that I can recall."

At the time, the Biological Survey was trying to kill all the predators, such as wolves and coyotes, in the area. Olaus's research showed that this was upsetting the natural balance of the area

Mardy and Olaus Murie dressed in parkas.
The Murie Center

and causing the herd to decline. His work at saving the elk herd caused him to become known as "Mr. Elk."

Mardy served on the school board in Jackson Hole and worked to support the schools and the local library. She and Olaus loved to dance, so they organized dances for the local teens.

In 1937 Olaus accepted a seat on the council of the Wilderness Society. Both he and Mardy worked with conservationists, including Aldo Leopold.

Olaus testified before Congress that the boundaries of Olympic National Monument were unnatural. He helped convince Franklin D. Roosevelt to add the rain forests of the Bogachiel and Hoh River Valleys to the national monument area. He and Mardy were also instrumental in creating Jackson Hole National Monument in 1943. A few years later, they helped make Grand Teton a national park. It included most of the Jackson Hole National Monument.

During World War II, Mardy volunteered at a hospital, bathing patients and scrubbing the floor of the operating room. She managed another couple's dude ranch for them and grew a victory garden.

In 1945 Olaus resigned from the Biological Survey. He was unhappy that they had ignored some of the findings of his research. He disagreed with the survey's policy of killing off all the predators. He said, "Poisoning and trapping of so-called predators and killing rodents, and the related insecticide and herbicide programs, are evidences of human immaturity. The use of the term 'vermin' as applied to so many wild creatures is a thoughtless criticism of nature's arrangement of producing varied life on this planet."

Olaus took a job as director of the Wilderness Society. "We had become immersed in the conservation battle," Mardy said, "and enthralled and stimulated by it and the interesting people we met in connection with them. . . . We both knew that life was blooming, expanding, growing because of the new work Olaus had undertaken. It demanded a great deal of both of us."

Robert Marshall, a founder of the Wilderness Society, was one of the first to suggest preserving large areas of Arctic Alaska. Olaus and Mardy took the lead in promoting the idea. Olaus said, "The Arctic Range should be kept for basic

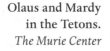

Olaus and Mardy in the Tetons.
The Murie Center

Grand Teton National Park

Grand Teton National Park is just south of Yellowstone in northwestern Wyoming. The park was originally created by Congress in 1929, but it was much smaller than it is now. It only included the Teton Mountain range and the eight lakes that lie at their base.

The park was increased to its present size in 1950. It now includes Jackson Hole and 35,000 acres of land donated by John D. Rockefeller Jr. The mountain range includes 12 peaks over 12,000 feet high. The tallest is Grand Teton, with an elevation of 13,770 feet.

Besides breathtaking scenery, the park is home to numerous species of plants and animals. Over 900 species of flowering plants are found there. Grand Teton is home to 17 species of carnivores, 4 species of reptiles, 5 species of amphibians, and over 300 species of birds.

The park includes several types of habitat. Alpine habitat is found above the treeline. A lot of the lower land is dry sagebrush flats. There are also forests, ponds, lakes, and rivers.

By the first of November, heavy snow begins to fall, closing most of the roads until at least March. From April until October, visitors enjoy driving the roads, hiking the trails, camping, and viewing wildlife.

Teton Mountains in Grand Teton National Park.

The Tundra

The Alaskan tundra is an interesting and unusual biome. Few trees grow there because of the short growing season and low temperatures. The average temperature in the tundra is about 40 degrees Fahrenheit (5 degrees Celsius.)

The Alaskan Tundra.
Library of Congress, LC-DIG-highsm-04828

Beneath the surface of the soil is permafrost, which is soil that is permanently frozen. Only the top 10 to 35 inches of the soil thaws out in the summer. When the upper layer of the soil thaws, the ground becomes very soggy. During the warm months, many lakes and marshes form. The temperature may get up to 54 degrees Fahrenheit (12 degrees Celsius) in summer. However, it can drop to below freezing at night.

In spite of the short growing season and low temperatures, the tundra is home to a wide variety of plants. Many wildflowers bloom in the summer. Lichens, mosses, sedges, and grasses are also found here.

Caribou, musk ox, snowy owls, lemmings, Arctic hares, and Arctic foxes live in the tundra. There are no reptiles or amphibians in the tundra, since they can't tolerate the extreme temperatures.

The tundra is threatened by oil development. Oil lies below the tundra, and many believe it should be extracted. Another threat to the tundra is global warming, which could change the kinds of species that live there. Also, when permafrost melts, carbon dioxide and methane are released into the air, causing more global warming.

Snowy owl.

Walking on the tundra damages the vegetation. It can take hundreds of years to repair the damage done by a few people walking across the tundra.

scientific study, for observation, as a help to us for our understanding of the natural processes in the universe."

In 1956, the Muries led several other field biologists on a summer-long expedition into the Arctic wilderness. They needed someone who was well-known to help promote the idea of saving this wilderness. Two years earlier, Olaus had hiked the 180-mile-long Chesapeake and Ohio Canal with Supreme Court Justice William O. Douglas. The group hiked from Washington, DC, to Cumberland, Maryland, in a successful effort to prevent turning the tow path into a highway. Douglas had impressed Olaus with his knowledge of birds and his support of conservation.

The Muries thought Douglas would be the perfect person to help with their campaign to save the Arctic wilderness. Douglas agreed to join the expedition to the Valley of Lakes on the Sheen-jak River. He insisted they call him Bill, and he joined in all the activities and chores. Mardy was impressed by his interest in everything around him—the plants, the birds, and the animals.

When he returned, Douglas wrote, "This is—and must forever remain—a roadless, primitive area where all food chains are unbroken, where the ancient ecological balance provided by nature is maintained."

He also wrote, "The beauty is in part the glory of seeing moose, caribou, and wolves living in a natural habitat, untouched by civilization. It is the thrill of seeing birds come thousands of miles to nest and raise their young. . . . The Arctic has a call

Olaus and Mardy.
The Murie Center

that is compelling. The distant mountains make one want to go on and on over the next ridge and over the one beyond. The call is that of a wilderness known only to a few. It is a call to adventure."

Douglas's writings and the photos and movies the Muries took were convincing. In 1960, President Eisenhower signed an executive order creating the Arctic National Wildlife Range (now known as the Arctic National Wildlife Refuge). It set aside 8.9 million acres in the northeastern corner of Alaska to forever remain a wilderness.

Mardy and Olaus then began campaigning for the passage of the Wilderness Act. Unfortunately, Olaus died a few months before it was passed. Mardy's son Donald said in an interview, "After my father's death, she didn't know what she was going to do. But when she returned from her travels, she said, 'I have to continue. I have to do this for Olaus.'"

Justice William O. Douglas

William O. Douglas served as a US Supreme Court justice for nearly 37 years. He was born in Minnesota, then his family moved to California. His father died when he was six, and his mother and her three children settled in Yakima, Washington.

William did well in high school and won a scholarship to Whitman College in Walla Walla, Washington. He earned a degree in English and economics. Then he taught for two years to save money for law school.

After law school, he taught at Columbia Law School, then at Yale Law School. Later, President Franklin D. Roosevelt nominated him to the US Securities and Exchange Commission. He became friends with the president.

When Justice Louis Brandeis resigned from the Supreme Court in 1939, Roosevelt nominated Douglas to replace him. Douglas was one of the youngest justices to be confirmed to the US Supreme Court.

He often disagreed with some of the other justices. He strongly defended the right of the people to free speech.

Douglas was an outdoorsman and a strong supporter of the environment. He served on the board of directors of the Sierra Club, wrote articles about the environment, and is credited with saving the Chesapeake and Ohio Canal. He backed Rachel Carson and her book *Silent Spring*. Douglas also published a paper called "Environmental Law."

Two unsuccessful attempts were made to remove him from his position as a justice. In 1974 he suffered a stroke that left him partially paralyzed. He was confined to a wheelchair and retired the next year.

Douglas when he was appointed to the Supreme Court.
Library of Congress LC-DIG-hec-26328

Murie served on the governing council of the Wilderness Society, and her home became the unofficial headquarters for the group. She wrote letters and articles, lectured, lobbied in Congress, and testified before congressional committees. She backed the Alaska National Interest Lands Conservation Act, which was signed by President Jimmy Carter in 1980.

In testimony before Congress she said, "I am testifying as an emotional woman, and I would like to ask you, gentlemen, what's wrong with emotion? Beauty is a resource in and of itself. Alaska must be allowed to be Alaska. . . . I hope the United States of America is not so rich that she can afford to let these wildernesses pass by, or so poor she cannot afford to keep them."

When this act passed, it doubled the size of the Arctic National Wildlife Refuge. A part of the coastal plain was still left "open for further study," which meant it could be used for mineral exploration. Oil drilling was already taking place in Alaska. The pipeline to carry the oil to the port of Valdez was opened in 1977. However, Arctic drilling became much less popular in 1989, after the *Exxon Valdez* oil spill.

When she was in her 90s, Murie was still living in the log cabin she and Olaus had built in the Grand Teton National Park. She enjoyed the moose and other animals surrounding her. A shy pine marten, an animal seldom seen by humans, raised several families under her cabin.

Murie received the Audubon Medal in 1980 and the John Muir Award from the Sierra Club in 1983. When President Bill Clinton awarded her the Presidential Medal of Honor in 1998, he said,

We owe much to the life's work of Mardy Murie, a pioneer of the environmental movement who, with her husband, Olaus, helped set the course of American conservation more than 70 years ago. Her passionate support for and compelling testimony on behalf of the Alaska Lands Act helped to ensure the legislation's passage and the protection of some of our most pristine lands. A member of the governing council of the Wilderness Society, she also founded the Teton Science School to teach students of all ages the value of ecology. For her steadfast and inspiring efforts to safeguard America's wilderness for future generations, we honor Mardy.

She told him, "Young man, there's still a lot of work to do."

Mardy passed the torch to the younger generation with her statement, "Every citizen has a responsibility toward this planet. I'm counting on the new generation coming up. I have to believe in their spirit as those who came before me believed in mine."

On October 19, 2003, Mardy died on her ranch at the age of 101. She left a huge legacy. She had written an autobiography, *Two in the Far North*, and two books with Olaus. Their home is now the headquarters of the Murie Center, an educational center dedicated to conservation.

Mardy Murie in her later years.
The Murie Center

TUNDRA DIORAMA

Using a shoebox or other similar box, you can make your own diorama to show people what the tundra is like.

WHAT YOU NEED

- Shoebox or similar box
- Colored paper or paint in various colors, including light blue
- Paintbrush, if you use paint
- Glue
- Several white Styrofoam meat trays, thoroughly washed with soap
- Scissors
- Loose soil or potting soil
- Small branch from an evergreen tree
- Tiny artificial flowers (optional)
- Plastic animals or heavy paper

WHAT YOU DO

1. Paint the outside of the box or cover it with colored paper.

2. Paint the inside of the box light blue or cover it with blue paper to represent the sky. Leave the side that will be the bottom of your diorama unpainted.

3. Cut enough flat pieces of Styrofoam to cover the bottom of the diorama. This will be the permafrost. Glue it down.

4. Pour an inch or so of soil on top of the permafrost.

5. Break off 1-inch-long pieces of evergreen branch to represent the dwarf pines that grow in the tundra. To "plant" them, poke a hole through the soil into the styrofoam. Dip the bottom of the twig in glue, then push it down into the hole.

6. The tundra is nearly covered with flowers in summer. Scatter tiny artificial flowers all over the ground, or make tiny paper flowers yourself and use those.

7. Add animals to your diorama. You can use plastic animals if you have them. Or you can draw animals on heavy paper and color them. Make a wide tab on the bottom of each paper animal for a base. Fold the tab under and put glue on the bottom. This should hold your animal upright. Another option is to draw or paint the animals on the back and sides of the inside of your diorama.

President Bill Clinton shakes hands with Mardy. *The Murie Center*

The Exxon Valdez Oil Spill

The *Exxon Valdez* was a huge oil tanker owned by the Exxon oil company. The ship carried oil from Valdez, Alaska, to other parts of the United States. Just after midnight on March 24, 1989, while trying to avoid icebergs, the ship ran aground on the Bligh Reef. Eight of the oil tanks were damaged, and oil began to spill into Prince William Sound.

Most of the oil was spilled in the first six hours. For a few days, the oil stayed together in one large patch near Bligh Island. On March 26, a storm with high winds spread the oil over a larger area. The high tides that are typical at that time of year deposited more oil on the shore.

People used hoses to spray seawater on the oil in an attempt to flush it off the beaches. They then tried to trap the oil and remove it. Many removal methods were tried, but none was very effective. Much of the oil remained 10 years later, and some is still there.

The oil spill had a huge impact on the ecosystem of Prince William Sound. This spill was considered one of the worst in history in terms of damage to the environment. One of the worst results was the harm to animals. An estimated 250,000 seabirds, 2,800 sea otters, 300 harbor seals, 250 bald eagles, and 22 killer whales died from the spill.

The ship was repaired and given a new name, the *Sea River Mediterranean*. It's now used to ship oil across the Atlantic Ocean. The tanker was banned from ever reentering Prince William Sound.

CLEANING UP AN OIL SPILL

In this activity, you'll try several different ways to clean up an oil spill. These are similar to the methods clean-up crews use to clean up an oil spill. See if any of them work well.

WHAT YOU NEED

- ❖ Large bowl
- ❖ Water
- ❖ Food coloring
- ❖ Cooking oil
- ❖ Measuring cup
- ❖ Paper towels
- ❖ Piece of string about 18 inches long
- ❖ Sponge
- ❖ Medicine dropper

WHAT YOU DO

1. Fill the bowl halfway with water. Add a few drops of food coloring to the water to help you better see the "oil spill" that you will put on top.

2. Pour ½ cup of cooking oil into a measuring cup.

3. Add the oil to the water. Shake the bowl and see if the oil and water mix.

4. Try to clean up the oil with a paper towel. How well does this work?

5. Make a border around the oil with the string and see if you can drag it to one side of the bowl. Does this work well?

6. Try to soak up the oil with a sponge. Does this work?

7. Use a medicine dropper to try to remove the oil from the water. Does this work?

RACHEL CARSON
1907-1964

Rachel Carson is best known as the author of *Silent Spring*, the book that led to a nationwide ban on DDT and spurred an environmental movement that led to the creation of the Environmental Protection Agency. *Silent Spring* has been described as a book that altered the course of history.

Rachel Louise Carson was born in the small town of Springdale, Pennsylvania. She lived with her parents and older brother and sister on a 65-acre farm near the Allegheny River. Rachel's mother wrote that she had taught her daughter "as a tiny child joy in the out-of-doors and the lore of birds, insects, and residents of streams and ponds." As a child, Rachel spent much of her time exploring nearby forests and streams.

Rachel read a lot and began writing stories when she was eight. When she was 10, her first story was published in

Rachel Carson.

St. Nicholas Magazine. She attended Springdale School through tenth grade, then went to nearby Parnassus, Pennsylvania, to finish high school. In 1925, she graduated at the top of her class.

That fall, Carson entered Pennsylvania College for Women. She majored in English so she could become a writer. When she took a required course in biology, she decided to switch her major. When she graduated from college, she won a scholarship to do graduate work at Johns Hopkins in Baltimore.

But before Carson went to Baltimore, she spent six weeks working at the Marine Biological Laboratory in Woods Hole, Massachusetts. There she served as a "beginning investigator in research." She was delighted with the research library there, where she found books and research journals from around the world. She did research on the cranial nerves of reptiles, which are nerves attached to the stem of the brain. She would use the information she collected to write her master's thesis at Johns Hopkins.

When she started at Johns Hopkins, Carson rented a house. Since she'd never been away from her family and wouldn't have had enough money to go home and visit, her parents moved in with her. Her brother, sister, and two nieces stayed in the farmhouse in Pennsylvania.

For the next four years, Carson taught summer school at Johns Hopkins while she finished her master's degree. She started work on her doctorate, but had to drop out due to lack of money.

(*left*) Rachel Carson as a child, reading to a dog.
Rachel Carson Council

(*right*) Carson at Marine Biological Laboratory at Woods Hole.
Lear/Carson Collection

In 1935, Carson's father died of a heart attack. Now Carson was the sole support of her mother and herself. She also helped her sister, Marian, and Marian's daughters. Rachel taught part-time at the University of Maryland, but she needed a full-time job, and jobs were hard to find during the Depression. She finally was offered a part-time job with the US Bureau of Fisheries. Her task was to write a series of 52 short radio programs on life in the sea. The program was called *Romance Under the Waters.* She was paid $6.50 a day.

The radio show was a big success, and when she was finished, Rachel's boss asked her to write an introduction to marine life to be used as a government brochure. While working on that, she sent off an article to the local newspaper, the *Baltimore Sun.* They published it and paid her $20.

When Carson finished the brochure, which she called "The World of Water," she showed it to her boss. He said, "I don't think it will do. Better try again." Then with a twinkle in his eye, he said, "But send this one to the *Atlantic.*" She stuck what she had written in a drawer and wrote a shorter, simpler brochure. She entered the original essay in a *Reader's Digest* contest, but never heard from them.

In July 1936, Carson got a job as a junior aquatic biologist with the Bureau of Fisheries. Only one other woman worked for the bureau on a professional level. Carson enjoyed her work and learned a lot about the fish in the area.

Carson began sending out more articles to magazines. During the first half of 1937, she sold at least seven articles. She used the research she did on the job to write the articles.

Rachel Carson needed to spend a lot of time in Washington, DC, and travel was expensive, so she rented a house in Silver Spring, Maryland, for the family. In January 1937, Rachel's sister died. Her daughters, Virginia, 12, and Marjorie, 11, moved in with Rachel and her mother. They needed more money, so Rachel dug out "The World of Water" and sent it to *Atlantic Monthly.* She soon heard from the editor, who wanted to publish it. She made a few revisions, and it was published in September with the title "Undersea." She received $100.

In 1939, Carson was promoted. She was now an assistant aquatic biologist with a salary of $2,600 a year. She was put in charge of all the laboratory and field reports. She also wrote descriptive material for brochures for the public.

Rachel continued writing other material outside of work. Her first book, *Under the Sea Wind,* was published in 1941. It received good reviews, but the bombing of Pearl Harbor and America's entry into World War II filled everyone's minds.

For the next 10 years, Carson continued to work for the bureau and to write articles. She also wrote a new book. Because of all her responsibilities with work and the family, it took a long time. She said, "I am a slow writer, enjoying the stimulating pursuit of research far more than the drudgery of turning out manuscript."

The second book, *The Sea Around Us,* amazed her with its popularity. It was on the *New York*

SALT WATER TO DRINKING WATER

The Earth has much more salt water than fresh water. But salt water can be changed into fresh water, suitable for drinking.

WHAT YOU NEED

- Measuring spoons
- Table salt
- Mixing bowl
- Measuring cup
- Water
- Mixing spoon
- Cup or mug
- Plastic wrap
- Small rock (about an inch wide)

WHAT YOU DO

1. Measure 1½ tablespoons of salt into the mixing bowl. Measure 3 cups of water and pour it into the mixing bowl. Stir until all the salt is dissolved.

2. Place the cup or mug in the center of the bowl. Be careful not to get any of the salty water in it.

3. Cover the bowl with plastic wrap and seal the edges tightly.

4. Place the small rock on top of the plastic wrap, just above the cup, so that it makes the plastic slant toward the cup.

5. Set the bowl carefully in the hot sun. Check it in an hour. Water droplets should be forming on the underside of the plastic and dripping into the cup.

6. After several hours, remove the plastic. You should find a good amount of water in the cup.

7. Taste the water in the cup. It won't be salty. The heat of the sun causes the water to turn into a gas, which rises to the cooler plastic wrap and turns back into liquid water. Salt does not evaporate, so it remains behind in the salt water.

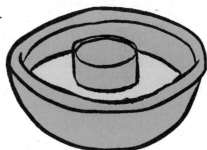

Times bestseller list for 86 weeks and was eventually translated into 33 languages. The *New York Times* wrote, "Great poets from Homer down to Masefield have tried to evoke the deep mystery and endless fascination of the ocean, but the slender, gentle Miss Carson seems to have the best of it."

Being a shy, serious person, Carson at first was terrified by all the attention. However, she learned to deal with it. She answered every piece of mail she received. Her ability to transform scientific facts into delightful description made her books interesting.

This book did so well that Carson was able to retire in 1952 and spend all her time on her writing. With some of the money from the book, she was able to fulfill two longtime dreams. She bought a binocular microscope and a summer cottage on the coast of Maine. She wrote another book, *Edge of the Sea,* which was published in October 1955. She was now a well-known author, and this book received good reviews.

Carson continued writing articles. In 1956, her niece Marjorie died at the age of 31. She left a son, Roger, who was five. Rachel adopted him. She now was caring for a little boy and an aging mother, as well as writing.

In 1958, Carson received a letter from a friend in Massachusetts. The woman was concerned because many large birds on Cape Cod had died as a result of people using the insecticide DDT. As early as 1945 Rachel had been concerned about the pesticide and proposed an article on it to *Reader's Digest.* They turned it down. Now her interest was rekindled.

Carson spent four years researching the book she decided to write. DDT had been introduced during World War II to kill the mosquitoes and

(*left*) Rachel Carson and Bob Hines doing marine biology research in Florida.
US Fish and Wildlife Service

(*right*) Rachel Carson doing field work.
US Fish and Wildlife Service

Earth Day

Gaylord Nelson, founder of Earth Day, says he is often asked how Earth Day started and what its purpose was. At the time of the first Earth Day in 1970, Nelson was a Democratic US senator from Wisconsin. He said the idea for Earth Day came about over a period of seven years, after he read Rachel Carson's *Silent Spring.* He tried to promote environmental issues and got President Kennedy to go on a national five-day conservation tour. It wasn't as effective as he had hoped.

Senator Nelson continued to speak on environmental issues all across the country. He says the people seemed concerned, but politicians weren't. He witnessed anti–Vietnam War demonstrations called "teach-ins," and something clicked. He decided he would organize a nationwide protest to bring attention to issues with our environment.

With the help of Republican Congressman Pete McCloskey and environmentalist Denis Hayes, who agreed to be national coordinator, Nelson spread the word. On April 22, 1970, 20 million Americans across the country demonstrated for a healthy environment. Thousands of colleges and universities organized protests against the deterioration of our environment.

The first Earth Day marked the beginning of the modern environmental movement. It led to the passage of the Clean Air Act and the Clean Water Act and the creation of the EPA. Earth Day is now celebrated every spring, with more than a billion people all over the world participating.

other insects that caused malaria and typhus in our troops abroad. It was very successful, and Paul Herman Muller, a Swiss chemist, won the Nobel Prize in 1948 for his discovery of its effectiveness.

At the time, no one knew the chemical had side effects that were dangerous to animals and humans. They also didn't realize that insects would soon become immune to it.

Carson's studies had shown the effects of DDT on marine life. She was not alone in her worries. Edward Way Teale wrote, "A spray as indiscriminate as DDT can upset the economy of nature as much as a revolution upsets social economy. Ninety percent of all insects are good and if they are killed, things go out of kilter right away."

As she wrote the book, Rachel was suffering from cancer. However, she kept up her research and writing. DDT was now being sprayed from planes in order to fight Dutch Elm disease. There was evidence that robins were dying from eating earthworms poisoned by the spray on the leaves of the trees.

Silent Spring was published in 1962. The book provoked immediate controversy. The pesticide industry attempted to have the book taken off the market. They tried their best to discredit Carson, calling her a "hysterical female." They took out ads telling the American public to ignore the book. Dr. Robert White-Stevens, speaking for the chemical industry, said,

> The major claims of Miss Rachel Carson's book, *Silent Spring*, are gross distortions of the actual facts, completely unsupported by scientific, experimental evidence, and general practical experience in the field. Her suggestion that pesticides are in fact biocides destroying all life is obviously absurd. . . . The real threat, then, to the survival of man, is not chemical but biological, in the shape of hordes of insects that can denude our forests, swoop over our crop lands, ravage our food supply, and leave in their wake a train of destitution and hunger, conveying to an undernourished population the major disease scourges of mankind.

Still, many Americans believed what Carson had written and flooded Congress and the president with letters demanding something be done about DDT. President Kennedy asked for a special committee of scientists to investigate the claims made in the book. Congress also set up an investigative committee.

Carson remained calm. She defended her research and told Americans to "think for themselves." She said we needed to think about the

(*left*) President John F. Kennedy.
Library of Congress
LC-USZ62-117124

(*below*) Planes like this were used to spray DDT.
Library of Congress
LC-USF33-005005-M2

The Environmental Protection Agency

The EPA came into being on December 2, 1970. It combined the duties of a number of other organizations. President Nixon appointed 38-year-old William D. Ruckelshaus as its first director, and he was confirmed by the US Senate on December 1. He already had an impressive record in government.

According to Nixon, the mission of the EPA included:

❖ The establishment and enforcement of environmental protection standards consistent with national environmental goals.

❖ The conduct of research on the adverse effects of pollution and on methods and equipment for controlling it; the gathering of information on pollution; and the use of this information in strengthening environmental protection programs and recommending policy changes.

❖ Assisting others, through grants, technical assistance, and other means, in arresting pollution of the environment.

❖ Assisting the Council on Environmental Quality in developing and recommending to the president new policies for the protection of the environment.

The EPA's strength was tested early in January 1971. Ruckelshaus rejected a plan submitted by Union Carbide to reduce emissions from their plant in Marietta, Ohio. Union Carbide threatened to lay off 625 workers. The EPA managed a compromise that saved the workers' jobs and still reduced emissions by 70 percent in a little over a year.

The Clean Air Act was passed on December 31, 1970. This act set national standards for auto emissions, air quality, and pollution. According to the EPA, it prevented over 200,000 deaths in the first 20 years after its passage by reducing the presence of harmful pollutants such as lead and sulfur dioxide in the air.

The Clean Water Act, passed in 1972, has made our drinking water safer. The EPA has also banned DDT, protected our oceans and lakes from toxic dumping, added to our understanding of global warming and greenhouse gases, and much more.

Administrator Lisa Jackson has set the following seven priorities for the EPA's future:

1. Taking action on climate change

2. Improving air quality

3. Insuring the safety of chemicals

4. Cleaning up our communities

5. Protecting America's waters

6. Building strong state and tribal partnerships

7. Expanding the conversation on environmentalism and working for environmental justice

future and the kind of world we would leave for our children. She also said, "We must have insect control. I do not favor turning nature over to insects. I favor the sparing, selective and intelligent use of chemicals. It is the indiscriminate, blanket spraying that I oppose." She was asked to testify before the Congressional committee, and told them, "I deeply believe that we in this generation must come to terms with nature."

In 1963 CBS aired *CBS Reports: The Silent Spring of Rachel Carson*. In the program Carson said, "Man's attitude toward nature is today critically important simply because we have now acquired a fateful power to alter and destroy nature. But man is part of nature, and his war against nature is inevitably a war against himself. . . . Now, I truly believe, that we in this generation must come to terms with nature, and I think we're challenged as mankind has never been challenged before to prove our maturity and our mastery, not of nature, but of ourselves."

Kennedy's commission supported Carson's findings. Congress made a number of laws that banned or controlled dangerous pesticides. They also called for more careful testing of the side effects of these chemicals.

In 1970 Congress created the Environmental Protection Agency (EPA). In 1972 they banned the use of DDT. Sweden had banned the chemical in 1969 when scientists there discovered that the pesticide had contaminated human milk.

Sadly, Rachel Carson did not live to see some of these changes go into effect. She lost her battle with cancer on April 15, 1964, at her home in Silver Springs, Maryland. Her great-nephew, Roger, was 11 years old. Her friends Paul and Susie Brooks took him in and finished raising him, as Carson had asked in her will.

Carson and *Silent Spring* brought environmentalism to the attention of the average American. Before she wrote the book, the destruction of nature was described as progress. *Silent Spring* introduced the term *ecosystem* to the world.

Carson had gone about her writing and her research quietly, but her work had a tremendous

The Wells National Estuarine Research Reserve at the Rachel Carson National Wildlife Reserve. *Library of Congress LC-HS503-6742*

impact on the environment. Former vice-president Al Gore says her work is responsible for the creation of the EPA. He said that *Silent Spring* helped him and millions of others develop an environmental consciousness.

Carson received many awards, some of them after her death. She was awarded the Gold Medal of the New York Zoological Society, the John Burroughs Medal, the Gold Medal of the Geographical Society of Philadelphia, and the National Book Award.

The Rachel Carson Reserve, located near Cape Lookout on the coast of North Carolina, is named for her. The site includes many habitats, including tidal flats, ocean beach, sand dunes, and maritime forest. More than 200 species of birds have been observed here.

11

ROGER TORY PETERSON
1908-1996

Roger Tory Peterson's biggest contribution to environmentalism was his system of bird identification. By using his system, anyone could identify live birds in the wild. This was the beginning of the popular hobby of birding.

Peterson was born in Jamestown, New York, on August 28, 1908. His father, Charles Gustav Peterson, was an immigrant from Sweden. His mother, Henrietta Bader, had come from Germany. At the time of Roger's birth, woolen mills provided most of the jobs in Jamestown. The Swedish craftsmen made it into a city of furniture factories.

Roger's father began work in the woolen mills at age 10 to help support his family after his father died. He only had a third-grade education. As a child, Roger resented his father

Roger Tory Peterson.

Northern flicker.
Dover Publications, Inc.

and used nature to teach science, art, and writing. Roger began studying, photographing, and drawing birds. Then he started painting them.

Roger was hiking one Saturday morning and saw what looked like a clump of feathers in a tree. It was a northern flicker. Thinking it was dead, Roger said, "I poked it with a stick and it burst into colors, with the red on the back of its head and the gold on its wing. It was the contrast, you see, between something I thought was dead and something so alive. Like a resurrection. . . . It made me more aware of the world in which we live."

As a boy, Roger got a job delivering newspapers so he could buy a camera to photograph birds. He wrote, "I . . . saved enough for a four by five inch plate camera, a Primo No. 9, that cost me somewhat more than $100, a lot of money in those days." He used the camera only to photograph birds. He didn't even take pictures of his friends.

Roger's first published photo, of northern cardinals, appeared in the 1925 Jamestown High School yearbook. The next year, they used his photo of black-capped chickadees.

Roger's best grades in high school were in art, history of art, and mechanical drawing. He graduated at the age of 16. Next to his picture in the yearbook was written, "Woods! Birds! Flowers! Here are the makings of a great naturalist!" Whoever wrote that was right.

His first job in the summer of 1925 was at the Union National Furniture Company. He made $8 a week painting Chinese designs on fancy

and thought he was hard on him. Mr. Peterson also didn't understand Roger's interest in nature. But his mother did. She made him a butterfly net and went to the druggist to get cyanide for him so he could preserve insect specimens.

The other children didn't understand Roger, either. He had skipped two grades, so he was younger than his classmates. They weren't interested in nature and called him "Professor Nuts Peterson." Since the other children thought he was strange, Roger was a loner, content to enjoy nature by himself.

When Roger was in seventh grade, his teacher, Blanche Hornbeck, got her students to join the Junior Audubon Club and taught them about birds. She often took them to the woods wood cabinets. His boss, William von Langereis, encouraged him to become an artist and insisted he enroll in art school.

Roger worked and saved his money for two years. During those two years, he practiced drawing, painting, and photographing birds. He spent hours at the library in Jamestown researching nature.

In 1927 Peterson began studies at the Art Students League in New York City. Two years later, he went on to the National Academy of Design. He also read magazines about birds, including *The Auk* (journal of the America Ornithological Union), *Wilson's Bulletin* (journal of the Wilson Ornithological Society), *Bird Lore* (National Audubon Society Magazine), and *National Geographic*.

Peterson read a notice in *The Auk* about a bird art show at the American Museum of Natural History. He submitted two paintings and both were accepted. The next year two of his paintings were displayed at Cooper Ornithological Club's first American Bird art exhibit at their annual meeting in Los Angeles. At only 17, he was already exhibiting his paintings with the great bird artists of the time.

When Peterson graduated from the National Academy of Design in 1931, he got a job teaching science and art at a private day school. The Rivers Country Day School in Brookline, Massachusetts, was a prep school for wealthy boys. He taught there for three years. One of his students was Elliot Richardson, who later became attorney general of the United States. Richardson said Peterson was the teacher who influenced him the most.

During the summers, Peterson served as a nature counselor. He worked first at a YMCA camp in Michigan. Then he spent five summers working at Camp Chewonki in Maine.

In 1929, Bill Vogt, editor of *Bird Lore Magazine*, suggested to Peterson that he write a field guide to birds. Peterson began working on one. It was rejected by three New York publishers. Finally, Houghton Mifflin, a small publisher in Boston, agreed to publish the book. They would print 2,000 copies, but he wouldn't get any royalties on the first thousand.

In less than three weeks, the books were all sold. Roger received 10 cents apiece on the second thousand books—$100. The book and its later editions have since sold over seven million copies.

The American Museum of Natural History in New York City. *Library of Congress LC-D4-71386*

THE PETERSON IDENTIFICATION SYSTEM

Learn to identify eight birds in your backyard or at a nearby park using the Peterson Identification System.

WHAT YOU NEED

- ❧ Binoculars (helpful, but not absolutely necessary)
- ❧ Pencil and paper
- ❧ A Roger Tory Peterson Field Guide (check one out from the library)

WHAT YOU DO

1. Find a bird.

2. Look at its shape and size.

3. Look at its color.

4. Notice field marks, such as a ring around the eye, bars on the wings, or a notch in the tail.

5. Write down these observations before you look in the book. Then if the bird flies away you won't have to think, "Oh, what color was the head?" or "Did it have wing bars?"

6. Look through the book and try to identify the bird.

7. It helps if you can tell what general family the bird fits into. Is it a duck? Is it an owl? Is it a small songbird? These families of birds are grouped together.

8. When you find a bird that looks like the one you're looking for, check its size, shape, and color. Notice the little arrows. They point to the most important field marks.

9. You may want to start keeping a list of all the birds you see. Birders call this a life list.

What made the book so popular was the Peterson Identification System. Using this system, anyone could identify live birds in the wild. Before this book came out, birds were identified through a series of measurements and observations of dead specimens.

Peterson said, "I grouped birds that looked alike and therefore might be mistaken for each other, instead of grouping them by species. I . . . drew little arrows to point out the 'field marks' that are the main information you need to identify a bird. Those arrows were my invention."

His descriptions are short and simple but very useful in learning to identify birds. For example, he wrote about the male American goldfinch—"The only small yellow bird with black wings." Anyone who learns that description can easily identify a goldfinch flying by.

After the book was published, Peterson took a job in New York as art editor and educational specialist for *Audubon Magazine*. He began working on other field guides, and the series now totals 52 books.

His son, Lee Peterson, described how his father worked. "Dad always likened writing a field guide to serving a prison sentence. . . . When he was working full-bore, he would work around the clock . . . his focus and intensity at work were phenomenal. . . . As for my brother, Tory, and I, there were days we might only see him at the breakfast or dinner tables or hear him return from the studio in the middle of the night."

American goldfinch.

Peterson began writing articles on birds and other topics. He loved to teach about the importance of using the environment wisely.

During World War II, he served in the Air Corps from 1940 to 1943. He was asked to write a plane-spotting training manual. Because people were successful at identifying birds with his field guide, the Air Corps believed he could adapt his system to teach the identification of planes.

After the war, Peterson spent the next 50 years writing, painting birds, and photographing birds. His work appeared in *National Geographic, Field and Stream, Ranger Rick, Life, Audubon, Nature*, and *Reader's Digest*. Much of his time was spent writing field guides on all kinds of topics, from insects, to animal tracks, to wildflowers.

(*above*) Peterson photographing
birds for a field guide.
© *Bob Krist/CORBIS*

(*right*) President Jimmy Carter.
Library of Congress LC-U9- 39080B-11A

For the last 30 years of his life, he and his wife, Virginia, traveled and worked together on the field guides.

The Roger Tory Peterson Institute of Natural History in Jamestown, New York, was dedicated on August 29, 1993, the day after Peterson's 85th birthday. He attended, and the crowd sang "Happy Birthday" to him.

Peterson won many awards, including the Conservation Medal of the National Audubon Society, the Gold Medal of the World Wildlife Fund, and awards from the Swedish and the Dutch. In 1980 President Jimmy Carter awarded him the Presidential Medal of Freedom.

Peterson actively wrote, photographed, and painted to the very end. His stepdaughter, Mimi Westervelt, described him taking a photo. She said,

At age 87, he's crouched down, camera to his eye, in some brush along a wetland focusing on a butterfly. He's just walked through some thorny mass of greenbrier or thistle or multiflora rose and his legs and arms are all scraped up, but he never mentions it. Because he doesn't feel it. His head and neck are thick with insects, but he never flinches. Because he doesn't feel them. He doesn't see them. He doesn't hear them. All he sees is that butterfly. As long as he hadn't just run out of film, Roger knew how to focus.

Peterson summed up his beliefs by saying, "The philosophy that I have worked under most of my life is that the serious study of natural history is an activity which has far-reaching effects in every aspect of a person's life. It ultimately makes people protective of the environment, in a very committed way. It is my opinion that the study of natural history should be the primary avenue for creating environmentalists."

Peterson died on July 29, 1996, soon after Mimi wrote this observation. He was still working on the fifth edition of *A Field Guide to the Birds of Eastern and Central North America* when he passed away, as well as several other projects. His wife, Virginia, said that the morning of his death he was working on a painting of flycatchers for the book. The plate with the unfinished paintings was included in the field guide.

The *New York Times* announced his death, referring to him as "the best-known ornithologist of the twentieth century." *Sports Afield* called him "the twentieth century's most influential naturalist." Paul Erlich wrote in *The Birders' Handbook*, "In this century, no one has done more to promote an interest in living creatures than Roger Tory Peterson, the inventor of the modern field guide."

Peterson made it possible for the average person to identify birds in the wild and to enjoy the hobby of birding. But he promoted all of nature through his field guides on almost every natural history topic. His challenge to those of us left on Earth is to help to sustain the natural order in the world as well as to recognize its beauty.

The Presidential Medal of Freedom

The Presidential Medal of Freedom is the highest award given to civilians by the United States. The recipients are chosen by the president.

In 1945, President Harry Truman established a Medal of Freedom to reward civilians who served during World War II. In 1963, President John F. Kennedy established the current award. The same person can receive the medal more than once. It can also be awarded posthumously.

A number of environmentalists have received the medal. They include Jacques Cousteau, Rachel Carson, Mardy Murie, Marjorie Stoneham Douglas, and Roger Tory Peterson. The medal was also awarded to Gaylord Nelson for his part in establishing Earth Day.

12

WHERE DO WE GO FROM HERE?

As you've seen in this book, much has already been done to help the environment. However, we still have a long way to go toward cleaning up and learning to take care of our environment. What follows are descriptions of some of the main problems that still face us, what can be done about them, and who is working on finding solutions.

ENERGY SOURCES

The burning of fossil fuels such as gas, oil, and coal causes many problems for our environment. When these fuels are burned, they pollute the air. Much has been done to clean up the pollution caused by fossil fuels, but other forms of energy that don't cause air pollution are available.

Wind turbines.

Fossil fuels are also nonrenewable. That means that once they're gone, they're gone. There won't be any more to use. The United States has many deposits of coal, oil, and gas, but some are hard to access. This has caused us to turn to foreign countries to buy oil.

The United States has also turned to offshore drilling in order to access the oil deposits under the ocean. This has had tragic results in a number of cases, the most recent being the BP oil spill in April 2010.

Alternative sources of energy are cheaper and don't pollute the environment. These include solar energy, wind power, and hydroelectric power.

Solar energy is one of the most promising. Solar energy comes from the sun, which each year releases about 35,000 times the amount of energy we use. It can be used to heat homes, power factories, and run cars.

Wind energy is another good source of energy that will not harm the environment. The energy is generated by windmills and is used to make electricity. Windmills are dependent on weather and climate, so they need to be placed where wind is common. But care must be taken not to locate windmills along flyways used by millions of birds for their twice-yearly migration. Otherwise, many birds will be killed by flying into the windmills' rotating blades.

Nuclear energy is another option available to us. However, it has its dangers. In 2011, Japan's worst earthquake caused the nuclear plant at Fukushima to lose power. Workers couldn't pump water to cool the atomic core, so they had to vent radioactive steam into the air to release the pressure. A number of explosions then blew out the concrete walls around the reactors. More than 200,000 people had to be evacuated because of the high radiation levels. Engineers will need to come up with strategies to make nuclear energy safer before it will become widespread.

DEFORESTATION

Deforestation is the clearing of large forests of trees. Trees are important because 70 percent of the Earth's plants and animals live in the forests. When their habitat is destroyed, many of them become endangered.

Clear-cutting forests also contributes to global warming. Trees help to hold moisture in the earth. They also absorb carbon dioxide, which

Deforestation in Colorado.
Library of Congress
LC-USF34-037708-D

helps to combat the greenhouse effect and global warming.

The best way to solve this problem would be to simply stop cutting trees. However, this probably won't happen. Areas of trees are cleared every day to provide room for homes, shopping centers, and businesses. Also, the lumber from trees is used for building, making paper, and many other things. Managing the forests, as Gifford Pinchot and Aldo Leopold urged, is the best way to combat deforestation. New trees must be planted to replace the ones that have been cut. This is being done in some areas, but not nearly enough trees are being planted to replace the ones that are cut.

For years, we've heard the cry, "Save the rainforest!" This is another side of deforestation. Much of the rainforest is still being destroyed by logging, agriculture, and fire. It is predicted that by 2030, half the Amazon rainforest will have been destroyed or severely damaged. Global warming plays a part in rainforest destruction. Global warming causes reduced rainfall, which can destroy the wildlife living in the rainforest.

GLOBAL WARMING

Global warming means that the Earth is gradually getting warmer. Adding greenhouse gases, such as carbon dioxide, to the atmosphere causes global warming. These gases build up in the atmosphere and cause heat that would otherwise escape into space to be trapped near the Earth.

An area of reforestation in Maryland.
Library of Congress
LC-DIG-fsac-1a34436

It may not sound like it would be a bad thing for the Earth to get warmer. However, this warming can cause a lot of problems. The warmer climate is causing the ice caps at the Arctic and the Antarctic to melt. This can make the level of the ocean rise, causing erosion and flooding along the shore. Scientists predict that sea level could rise as much as two feet during this century.

The white ice caps reflect a lot of sun away from the Earth. With less white ice and more dark water, more of the sun's heat will be absorbed. This is causing the permafrost to melt. Permafrost is frost under the ground in the Arctic that ordinarily stays frozen all year round. When it melts, it releases gases such as methane and carbon dioxide into the air, which causes more global warming.

The rate of global warming can be slowed down if people will take a few simple steps. It's

RAINFOREST SMOOTHIE

You can make a delicious smoothie using products from the rainforest.

WHAT YOU NEED

Adult supervision required

- 4 ice cubes
- Blender
- Measuring cup
- 1 cup orange juice
- Banana
- ½ cup pineapple
- Cut-up papaya or mango (optional)
- 2 glasses

WHAT YOU DO

1. Put the ice cubes in the blender.

2. Add the orange juice, banana, and pineapple. Add the mango or papaya if you wish.

3. Put the top on the blender and turn it on high. Let it run until the ice cubes turn to slush.

4. Pour the smoothie into two glasses and share with a friend.

necessary to reduce carbon emissions, 20 percent of which in the United States come from cars and trucks. People can help by carpooling, using public transportation, walking or bicycling, and limiting the number of trips they make. Deforestation and changing land use also causes 15 percent of our carbon emissions.

POLLUTION

Although much has been done to lessen the pollution of our air and water, we still have more work to do. Many laws have been created that prevent dumping factory wastes into streams and rivers. Water pollution damages plants and animals that live in bodies of water. It can also harm people if they drink the water

Acid rain occurs when too much carbon dioxide, sulfur dioxide, and nitrogen oxide react with the water in the air to produce acids. Acid rain is bad for forests, fresh water, and soil. It can kill insects and small life-forms that live in water. It can also damage buildings and monuments made of stone.

Water pollution comes from two sources. Point sources are single sources that can be identified, such as a pipe from a factory. Pollution at nonpoint sources, on the other hand, does not come from a single place. Agricultural runoff is an example of a nonpoint source. A farmer puts fertilizer on his fields and, after a while, it contaminates the water in the field. It can run off into a body of water or soak into the ground, where it becomes part of the groundwater, the water below the surface.

Oil spills occasionally occur at offshore drilling stations. Although they don't happen often, they can be disastrous for the condition of the water when they do.

IT'S UP TO YOU

These are a few of the most important threats to our environment today, but there are many other problems as well. Caring for our environment is going to take many people working together. Will you be one of those who helps?

Al Gore

Al Gore has done more than any other individual to bring the threat of global warming to the attention of the American people. Gore was vice-president of the United States under Bill Clinton from 1993 to 2001. Their administration cleaned up three times as many toxic waste sites as the Reagan and Bush administrations combined. They also passed clean air standards, which could save 15,000 lives a year. As a senator, Gore cosponsored the Water Quality Act of 1987.

In 2000 Gore ran for president against George W. Bush and lost in a contested election. After leaving office, he worked even harder. In 2006 Gore's book, *An Inconvenient Truth*, was released, along with a documentary film by the same name. Gore narrates the film, which follows a slide presentation he had given all over the world. It won an Academy Award and is the third most successful documentary ever released.

In 2007 Gore was awarded the Nobel Peace Prize for his efforts to make people aware of the threat of climate change. He's still working to inform people. In a speech in October 2011, Gore linked climate change to floods and other weather-related disasters around the world. He said, "We're still acting as if it's perfectly OK to use this thin-shelled atmosphere as an open sewer. It's not OK. We need to listen to the scientists. We need to use the tried and true method of using the best evidence, debating and discussing it, but not pretending that facts are not facts."

Some of Gore's critics accuse him of exaggerating claims about climate change. Many think his solutions will cost too much for big businesses to implement. However, most scientists back him up on his findings.

Al Gore.
Library of Congress
LC-HS503-5468

117

ACID RAIN

You can check rainwater to see if it contains acid.

WHAT YOU NEED

Adult supervision required

- ❁ 2 red cabbage leaves
- ❁ Knife
- ❁ 2 bowls
- ❁ Tap water
- ❁ Measuring cup
- ❁ Strainer or colander
- ❁ Permanent marker
- ❁ 2 small glass jars
- ❁ Distilled water (available at the grocery store)
- ❁ Rainwater (place a container in your yard to collect water when it rains)

WHAT YOU DO

1. Finely chop the cabbage leaves. Put them in one of the bowls.

2. Have an adult help you heat 1 cup of tap water and pour it over the cabbage leaves. Let it stand for an hour.

3. Pour the liquid through the strainer into the other bowl.

4. Use the marker to mark one jar with an R for rainwater and the other with a D for distilled water.

5. Measure ¼ cup of distilled water and pour it into the glass jar marked D. Measure ¼ cup of rainwater and pour it into the jar marked R.

6. Add ¼ cup of cabbage juice to each jar.

7. Compare the color of the water in the two jars. The color in the jar with the distilled water should stay the same. If there is acid in the rainwater, the water in that jar will turn red. The redder the water is, the more acid it contains.

RESOURCES

PLACES TO VISIT

Acadia National Park
25 Visitor Center Road
Bar Harbor, ME 04609
(207) 288-3338
www.nps.gov/acad
Cadillac Mountain, the tallest point on the Atlantic Coast, is within Acadia National Park. The park also has a wide variety of plant and animal life.

Crater Lake National Park
P.O. Box 7
Crater Lake, OR 97604
(541) 594-3000
www.nps.gov/crla
Crater Lake is actually a dormant volcano that has filled with water, creating a beautiful, deep blue lake. At 1,943 feet, it is the deepest lake in the United States.

Everglades National Park
4001 State Road 9326
Homestead, FL 33034
(305) 242-7700
www.nps.gov/ever
The Everglades once covered almost 11,000 square miles of Florida. About one-fifth of it has been protected as Everglades National Park. More than 350 species of birds have been sighted in the park, and over 40 species of mammals.

Grand Canyon National Park
2 Albright Avenue
Grand Canyon Village, AZ 86023
(928) 638-7888
www.nps.gov/grca
Over a period of 5 or 6 million years, the Colorado River cut a canyon more than a mile deep (6,000 feet). The canyon can be viewed from either the North or South Rim.

Grand Teton National Park

Cody Lane
Teton Village, WY 83025
(307) 734-7111
www.nps.gov/grte

Grand Teton National Park is located south of Yellowstone National Park. Moose, elk, bears, wolves, and bison roam the park. The Teton Mountains reach 13,770 feet in places.

Mesa Verde National Park

Cortez, CO 81321
(970) 529-4465
www.nps.gov/meve

The most prominent feature of Mesa Verde is the 600 cliff dwellings built by the Ancestral Pueblo Indians. They lived in these dwellings for over 700 years.

Mount Rainier National Park

55210 238th Avenue East
Ashford, WA 98304
(360) 569-2211
www.nps.gov/mora

Mount Rainier, an active volcano, rises 14,410 feet above sea level and contains the most glaciers of any US mountain outside of Alaska. The volcano last erupted about 150 years ago.

Petrified Forest National Park

1 Park Road
P.O. Box 2217
Apache, AZ 86028
(928) 524-6228
www.nps.gov/pefo

Petrified Forest National Park contains many sandstone mesas and buttes, but the most unusual feature in the park is the large number of petrified trees. Over the years, these logs have been turned to stone as the mineral silica replaced most of the wood.

Rachel Carson National Wildlife Refuge

321 Port Road
Wells, ME 04090
(207) 646-9226
www.fws.gov/northeast/rachelcarason

The refuge was established to protect the estuaries and salt marshes used every year by migrating birds. Threatened species here include the piping plover, the bald eagle, and the Northeastern cottontail rabbit.

Sequoia National Park

47050 Generals Highway
Three Rivers, CA 93271
(599) 565-3341
www.nps.gov/seki

Located on the edge of the Sierra Nevada Mountain Range, Sequoia National Park, together with Kings Canyon National Park, contains over 500 Native American archeological sites. The park is made up of huge sequoia trees, deep canyons, and high mountains.

Theodore Roosevelt National Park

315 2nd Avenue
Medora, ND 58435
(701) 623-4466
www.nps.gov/thro

Theodore Roosevelt's Elkhorn Ranch site is a part of the park and his first ranch home is open to visitors. The park is located in the Badlands, known for their layers of different colored rock. Many fossils are also found there.

Yosemite National Park

Northside Drive
Yosemite National Park, CA 95389
(209) 372-0200
www.nps.gov/yose

Yosemite National Park is famous for its waterfalls, mountains, and canyons. Half Dome and El Capitan are two of the best-known landmarks in the park. The Mariposa Grove, made up of giant sequoia trees, is also located in Yosemite.

BOOKS TO READ

Douglas, Marjory Stoneman. *Alligator Crossing*. Minneapolis: Milkweed Editions, 2003.

Hausman, Gerald and Loretta. *A Mind with Wings: The Story of Henry David Thoreau*. Boston: Trumpeter Books, 2000.

Hines, Gary. *Midnight Forests: A Story of Gifford Pinchot and Our National Forests*. Honesdale, PA: Boyds Mills Press, 2011.

Hunt, Nancy Nye. *Aldo Leopold's Shack: Nina's Story*. Chicago: Center for American Places, 2011.

Levine, Ellen. *Rachel Carson: A Twentieth Century Life*. New York: Viking Juvenile, 2007.

Malnor, Bruce and Carol. *Earth Heroes: Champions of the Wilderness*. Nevada City, CA: Dawn Publications, 2009.

Muir, John. Joseph Cornell, ed. *John Muir: My Life with Nature*. Nevada City, CA: Dawn Publications, 2000.

Murie, Margaret. *Two in the Far North*. Portland, OR: Alaska Northwest Books, 1997.

Rohmer, Harriet. *Heroes of the Environment: True Stories of People Who Are Helping to Protect Our Planet*. San Francisco: Chronicle Books, 2009.

Rothschild, David. *Earth Matters*. New York: DK Publishing, 2011.

Thomas, Peggy. *For the Birds: The Life of Roger Tory Peterson*. Honesdale, PA:Boyds Mills Press, 2011.

WEBSITES TO EXPLORE

Earth Day Kids' Activities
www.woojr.com/earth-day
This site contains all sorts of activities for Earth Day. It includes puzzles, coloring pages, and recycled craft projects. You can also sign up for a free kids' newsletter.

Ecokids Online
www.ecokidsonline.ca
The Ecokids site consists of a series of links to all kinds of kids' games, activities, and projects.

The Environment.net
http://the-environment.net/kids.html
The site has links to other kids' environmental sites, as well as having information on related topics, including nature, science, recycling, and wildlife.

The Environmental Protection Agency
www.epa.gov/students
Here you can learn about the environment while playing games and taking quizzes. There is a section on science fair projects and one on awards and contests for kids. And there are environmental videos you can watch.

Green Planet 4 Kids
http://greenplanet4kids.com
This site has comics explaining the conservation of water and electricity, plus a list of other websites.

INDEX

N

O

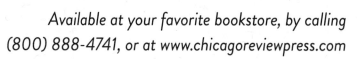 

978-1-56976-708-5
$12.95 (CAN $13.95)
Also available in e-book formats

SURVIVOR KID
A PRACTICAL GUIDE TO WILDERNESS SURVIVAL

DENISE LONG

"This practical book by a veteran search and rescue volunteer offers excellent tips on coping with potentially dangerous situations in the backcountry…a great book for anyone, young or old, who spends time in remote areas." —*Denver Post*

"A splendid volume for young adventurers." —*Kirkus Reviews*

"If exploring is on your child's agenda this summer, this is a great book to get lost in."
—*Queens Family* and *Brooklyn Family*

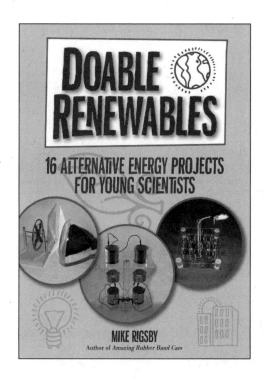

978-1-56976-343-8
$16.95 (CAN $18.95)
Also available in e-book formats

DOABLE RENEWABLES
16 ALTERNATIVE ENERGY PROJECTS FOR YOUNG SCIENTISTS

MIKE RIGSBY

"The focus on the hot topic of renewable energy . . . makes this a timely resource." —*Booklist*

"A useful book for larger collections." —*School Library Journal*

"Full of hands-on ways to help students understand the principles of alternative energy and have fun doing it." —*Curriculum Review*

Available at your favorite bookstore, by calling
(800) 888-4741, or at www.chicagoreviewpress.com

31901051914614